BLAST YOUR WAY TO MEGABUCK$ WITH MY *SECRET* SEX-POWER FORMULA

...and other reflections upon the spiritual path.
Being the second volume of the collected works of Ramsey Dukes, containing material in the 1980s (post Thundersqueak).

Edited By

Ramsey Dukes

Blast Your Way To Megabuck$ With My
Secret Sex-Power Formula.

Printed by New World Images, Doncaster, England.

Typesetting and Design by Thee Very Rev. Malchick Nostra

British Library Cataloguing in Publication Data

Cover designed by Steve Greaves M104

Concept by Ramsey Dukes

A CIP catalogue record for this book is available from The British Library.

ISBN 1 874171 02 5

CONTENTS

INTRODUCTION

In this volume and the forthcoming "What I Did In My Holidays" are collected all the essays and material that Ramsey Dukes has written post Thundersqueak - excluding the full-length book Words Made Flesh, and the forthcoming "The Good, The Bad and The Funny".

Although the first to be published, this is described as the "second volume" of collected works because it is intended to produce volume 1, containing the earlier material, at a later date. This seems a bit eccentric, but it reflects the harsh reality that the earlier material was not written on a word processor, and so has to be keyed in by hand when I can get round to it.

The material is included here in approximate chronological order, because it is of some interest to see how the ideas develop with time. The most obvious exception is the essay "Blast Your Way To Megabuck$" which was added later to give this volume a nice title. The first essay in this volume was written in 1980 and the last must have been about 1986 because it is a story derived from the book Words Made Flesh. Most of the articles have been published in magazines, and I am grateful for the chance to reproduce them here.

The next volume takes up essays written since Words Made Flesh and up to the time of publication. I know I've been promising this stuff for ages, but it only really became possible because Revelations 23 Press injected a shot of publishing competence into my shaky Mouse operation. So very grateful thanks, Mal.

Very often these essays were written in response to discussion with someone who has commented on earlier work, so I'd like to say "thank you" to all those who have inspired them!

1 - JOHNSTONE'S PARADOX

First Published in Arrow 8

This is the first of a series of articles about the theory I called "Johnston's Paradox'', and which was eventually written up in the Book "Words Made Flesh''. At the time I referred to "artificial intelligence" and "computer modelling" but currently the developing idea of "virtual reality" give's a better appreciation of the sort of "intelligent" interactive computer universe I am postulating.

The history of this idea is interesting from an astrological point of view. It first occurred to me in the Summer of 1980 at the time of a Jupiter Return - ie when transiting Jupiter was conjoined to its natal position in my horoscope. Jupiter is in my 9th house, appropriate to ideas. The idea of writing a book about it occurred in 1983/4, but I never managed to find the time until May 1986, by which time Jupiter was opposing its natal position. Having failed to find a publisher, I sent it to a printer myself in May 1988.

So far that represents a neat working out of the twelve-year Jupiter cycle: the idea is conceived at the conjunction, I want to write a book at the square, I do so at the opposition, it is published at the 9th house position... The next Jupiter return occurs for me in the year these essays are published.

Is there life elsewhere in the Universe?

The usual answer to this question is to argue that, although the probability of any one star system having the right conditions to support the creation of organic compounds might seem negligibly small, nevertheless the universe itself contains such a vast number of stars as to make the overall probability of life elsewhere very high.

The first extension of this argument is to say that, if the universe is infinite, then life elsewhere becomes absolutely certain. There is also a second, paradoxical extension which depends upon accepting the materialistic belief that all matter is based upon a finite number of elementary factors. In that case, although the probability of exactly reproducing our own world must seem too small to be worth considering, our existence proves the probability to be non-zero and so, in an infinite universe, this possibility again becomes absolutely certain. In other words, somewhere out in space there is a reader identical to yourself, reading this same article in an identical magazine. What is more this identical situation will be repeated indefinitely elsewhere in the universe.

The assumption of a finite number of elementary factors in matter is important to this paradox because, if we reject the materialist notion and accept that there could be an infinite subdivision of matter, then the probability of our own existence could dwindle to zero - and so the fact of our existence would demonstrate the action of a 'higher power' than probability.

It is this need for the double assumption of not only the finite basis of life, but also an infinite universe, that weakens the impact of this paradox and makes it inferior, in my mind at least, to what I call 'Johnstone's Paradox'.

Johnstone's paradox begins with the assumption of a mechanistic materialist universe. In such a universe we cannot bring in ideas of 'spirit' or 'etheric force' from outside, but instead must assume that everything we perceive is but a motion of matter. In that case it will become possible, when our computers are powerful enough, to program the entire structure of a human brain into a computer and so reproduce a human mind in 'mechanistic' though not necessarily 'deterministic' form. What must be realised is that we then will have not just a computer as 'clever' as a human, but one with the full human personality, dream life, and emotional and 'spiritual' nature - for what we call 'spirit' is, according to the basic assumption, no more than a by-product of the action of the human brain. (The arguments in support of this view are discussed more fully in Thundersqueak.)

The next step is to program into a computer not just one mind, but a whole society of human minds, together with all their perceptions of their environment, so that they can share a common 'dream' world within the computer. What must now be realised is that, although to us their world is a 'dream' world, to the people inside the dream it will seem utterly real. Provided sufficient data has been programmed in, and the computer's 'core' is sufficiently large, they will be able to communicate, fall in love, bear children, grow old and go on holiday all within that 'dream' world just as in the real world. If you think that this is impossible, then you are denying the mechanistic view of the world; either by saying that there are some elements of human existence which can never be reduced to codable information, or else by saying that the basic elements of existence are infinite and so could never by fully encoded.

In fact, the first steps in this direction have already been taken. Of course nothing so intricate as a human, or even an animal mind has been reproduced, but even by the early seventies simple dream worlds were being created. In Edinburgh they programmed a two-dimensional geometrical space in which a rudimentary 'mind' meandered around exploring its 'world', according to built-in 'laws of nature'. In Cambridge the mathematician Conway devised a two-dimensional 'game' called 'Life' which produced a growing and evolving pattern in the computer. He even raised the question as to whether he felt guilty when he switched the machine off!

What Johnstone suggested was that, if this process is indeed possible, then surely it will be done. What neater solution to the ultimate over-population problems, for example, then to recreate entire new universes in this way and disperse the people's 'souls' into this new level of reality? What greater art form could there be in a mechanistic world than to create a whole new universe or 'subuniverse' within a machine? The owner could at any point tune into this subuniverse and witness the rise and fall of cultures, individuals and races; lives of great heroism or tragedy would be there for the watching. Not only will this act of creation take place when it becomes possible, it will also take place a great many times. Our universe will then spawn a myriad sub-universes. The fact that this has already been done - though in a very complete and so far 'unreal' form - in the works of fiction writers adds force to the argument.

But what about the assertion with which this article began? Although there is speculation as to whether any intelligent beings exist within communicating distance of our solar system, the general assumption is that, in the universe as a whole, a very great number of highly advanced cultures must have developed. Amongst them many will be far beyond us in technical ability. In that case it becomes highly likely that the creation of subuniverses has already begun. In view of what was said earlier we should expect the number of these subuniverses to be very large, especially when we realise that within some of those subuniverses there will already be cultures sufficiently advanced to create sub- sub-universes...and so on...

So what Johnstone is suggesting is that, if the mechanistic world view is correct, then any one 'real' universe would spawn a huge number of subuniverses. In that case, using the probabilistic style of argument quoted earlier, it is very unlikely that our own universe should just happen to be a 'real' one - it is much more likely to be a subuniverse.

'What would be the nature of a typical subuniverse?' Johnstone asked. Surely it would not exactly duplicate the real universe? Only in the earliest stages of development would a highly evolved rational being be interested in reproducing another identical universe. The real interest would come from studying the result of making small changes in the basic structure. If the differences are too great then the subuniverse would contain beings so utterly different as to be incomprehensible and uninteresting. As with fantasy novels, the greatest interest would be in creating a universe with a lot in common with reality, and yet with certain fundamental differences.

So we would not expect the average subuniverse to obey identical laws to the real universe that contains it. In particular, if we assume the real universe to be utterly 'rational', it is highly probable that the average subuniverse would contain a small but significant element of 'irrationality'.

For example, we know from our initial assumption of a materialist world that there would be no such thing as reincarnation, so an obvious and economical experiment would be to create a world where the memory files of individuals are not totally erased on death, but are used as a basis for a future personality. As we know that mysticism would be rubbish it would be interesting to make it 'real' in our model. The synchronistic theory of divination - that all co-temporal events are linked - would not only be an interesting addition to the mechanistic model, it might also prove to be a much more economical use of computer time than a model which had to store a universe of random 'coincidences'. (In view of the assumed economy in nature that last point adds a special significance to the argument that will not be pursued in this short article). In other words we must add a little magic to our new universe to make it more exciting.

To summarise: we should perhaps not let ourselves be too limited by our present idea of what constitutes a 'computer', and simply say that a mechanistic universe, unlike some religious or magical universes, is one which would be utterly reproducible. Therefore we believe that it would reproduce. What is more it would reproduce indefinitely with indefinite more or less subtle variations from the original model. However, this multiplicity makes it extremely unlikely that we are privileged to be living in the original universe.

Putting the two parts of this argument together gives us Johnstone's Paradox, namely that: 'IF REALITY IS UTTERLY MECHANISTIC, IT IS HIGHLY UNLIKELY THAT WE ARE LIVING IN A MECHANISTIC UNIVERSE'.

I offer this as consolation in a world that is preparing for nuclear war. Or, as Crowley put it: AUMGN.

Perhaps some people will have little time for such a speculative argument as I have given, they will want it to be brought down to earth before they will feel it has any value.

A very good friend of mine and her husband began to experiment along the lines outlined in this article. Between them they have developed a small portable device with a view to creating such a new 'universe'. As I stated above, future developments may be along rather different lines from what we now call 'computers'. Sure enough, their device incorporates a sophisticated 'parallel processing' system, which means that in it large numbers of operations are performed simultaneously rather than in a linearly programmed form. It also incorporates video, audio, tactile and other sensors which provide the input for a general learning program. Provision has been made for extending facilities over the years but already the device has been given a certain amount of automotive power to explore 'the real world'. While it does this it is building up its own inner 'map' of the cosmos.

At first one might think that it can never complete this map until it has travelled and observed everywhere in the universe. This is overcome by a process of 'extrapolation'. For example it has learnt that its own house is made up of oblong rooms inside and has presumably noted a similar feature in all other houses visited. So, sooner or later, when it surveys a townscape, it will 'know' that all the visible buildings contain oblong rooms. Perhaps at a later date it will come across a trapezoidal or circular room and incorporate that possibility into its universe...and so on.

From the above example it can be seen that the device's inner world may deviate a little from 'reality'. My friend's husband has taken this into account by attempting to ensure that at least its 'world' will be an improvement on 'reality'. For example, he himself is prone to inferiority feelings and knows that nothing ever comes without a struggle - least of all gratitude. Accordingly he has made an unusual effort to pander to the device's needs - often rushing to solve its problems or extricate it from awkward situations before any 'distress' symptoms show. He hopes thereby to ensure that the fundamental 'world map' will be a benign one. This is of more than passing importance because all later experience will be processed within, and therefore coloured by, that fundamental map. As the device has early learnt that it gets what it wants it should later develop a 'success' type personality, unlike its creators.

Now basically I have no time for Johnstone's Paradox, for I have never been tempted to accept the mechanistic view. So, with tongue in cheek I drew up a horoscope for the moment when their device was first granted autonomy. Sure enough it had Sun, Mercury, Mars and Venus all in the first house! So I pointed out to the husband that he need not have tried so hard to compensate for his inadequacies, for his device was clearly bound to develop a powerful ego-sense despite his efforts! You might as well say it was his device's essential being which was inducing him to behave towards it the way he was, rather than say that his behaviour towards it was going to determine its essential being.

Not to be outdone by me he pointed out that this apparent inversion of cause and effect was much more in keeping with a universe which was being 'worked out' within a greater 'machine' than it was appropriate to our present ideas as to the nature of time and space. His little device was busy creating its own world out of fragments of our world, and was going about it in the same way as we developed our own universes in our own childhood. So we should respect its universe as much as our own, but try to allow it as much magic as we could.

In view of this example we can now see how this world we live in already contains several thousand million subuniverses. What is more we can observe that, however rational the 'reality' may be, an awful lot of those subuniverses are far from being themselves rational. We can also witness the evolution of those universes.

For example, those people who still believe in the traditional mechanistic universe are now growing increasingly dogmatic and cranky as their numbers dwindle. Perhaps the 'real' universe also evolves in this way? - after all it is hard to see how any civilisation living near the sea could ever have believed the world was flat in view of the evidence of their eyes. Most interestingly of all, perhaps, there is something in us that could direct the evolution of our own universe, e.g. to allow magic to grow in it despite our scientific culture. What does that directing, is it the machine itself or is it the ghost in the machine? Could it be that this True Will is so elusive because it is what remains when all that we now consider to be real has been stripped away?

Further research along these lines is up to the individual reader; for my friends, in keeping with the principles of Thundersqueak, have concealed the revolutionary nature of their work by conducting their experiments 'invisibly'. To all appearances their device described above is just a baby boy.

When I look around me and try to realise that all I see is a construct of past conditioning, and wonder what reality lies outside it all, then there are moments when I approach dizzily towards a new state of mind. That state somehow correlates with that curious inversion of Jung's VII Sermons Ad Mortuous, where the world of Gods and Demons is ascribed as the 'outer world'. Is this cold world around me then my 'inner' world? Are these the thoughts which 'estrangeth from being'?

2 - A NEW MUDDLE OF THE ONIVERSE (JOHNSTONE'S PARADOX, PART II)

First published in Arrow 9

The first Johnston's Paradox article was a bit terse for such a wide ranging idea, so I expanded it a lot for this one. But it was not until a later article (Johnstone's Paradox Re-visited) that I really began to explain it properly.

INTRODUCTION

In the last issue of Arrow I presented the argument for 'Johnstone's Paradox', which states that, if ultimate reality is as mechanistic as is suggested by the present-day anti-occult materialists, then it is extremely unlikely that we are living within such a reality. Or, if you prefer, 'magic is nonsense' implies that magic probably exists. The argument given might have seemed rather abstract to some readers so, in the second half of the article, I brought it down to earth with a more homely example.

Now I would like to extend this last step towards demonstrating how such apparently abstract philosophical speculations can impinge upon real life and be of help or inspiration to at least some occultists and magicians.

THE SHADOWS OF SCEPTICISM

I am sure that I am not alone in finding certain statements by self styled 'rationalist sceptics' very annoying. If an article on an occult topic is published in a fairly serious journal it tends to provoke an opposition which is blatantly dogmatic, obtuse, nit-picking or utterly blind to the facts. Such outbursts should be easy to dismiss, but many of us actually find them irritating. Why should trivial statements by apparently silly people upset us in this way?

In Liz Greene's latest book - with the off-puttingly down-market title of Star Signs for Lovers - she discusses the Jungian concept of 'the shadow' in astrological terms. In her earlier book on 'Saturn' she had pointed out how that planet can play the part of the shadow in a person's chart. In the latest book she further illustrates how each sign contains a certain 'shadow' potential according to its own nature. She also, in an introductory chapter, talks about one's 'shadow sign'. The 'shadow sign' is the polar sign to the sun-sign - ie, the sign opposite in the zodiac. She illustrates how any sun sign native can occasionally lapse into a nature corresponding to the worst features of the polar sign.

For example - under pressure the dynamic pioneering Aries man can reveal himself as an indecisive muddler who desperately wants to be liked (ie the lowest traits of Libra). In her book Liz Greene explains this in terms of the Jungian 'shadow' - an alternative way of saying the same thing might be to note that Sun in Aries in the usual geocentric system necessarily implies Earth in Libra in the more 'abstract' heliocentric system, and it is the non-recognition of this fact that leads to its negative 'shadow' manifestation.

For the sake of this essay I will limit myself to this last ingredient of the shadow - that polar nature which opposes one's normal expression and comes to be rejected and therefore autonomous. For illustrative convenience I will use the astrological terminology and ask: 'what characteristics do we associate with the rationalist scientific thinker?'

Without going too deeply into what is only intended to be a step in my argument I will suggest the following three factors as examples. a) The pure sceptical intellectualism of Gemini. b) The critical, down-to-earth discrimination of Virgo. c) The dispassionate iconoclasm and search for truth of Aquarius.

Taking these three examples, what characteristics might we expect from the 'shadow' of such thinkers? a) The pure logical 'game-playing' of Gemini could slip into the Sagittarian hunger to find connections - the search for one all-embracing principle. For example the behaviourist theory of psychology is no longer seen as a convenient tool for certain specific purposes, but it has to cover everything. b) The down-to-earth Virgo nature lapses occasionally into a Piscean escapist muddle. For example the sceptic who refuses to admit well documented occult phenomena, who turns a blind eye and hopes they will go away - 'I'm too busy to waste time on such obvious nonsense'; c) The individualistic, free-spirited Aquarian nature can lapse into a debased Leonine totalitarianism - having found its own truth it will force others to live by it.

Bearing in mind that I am not making any absolute statements about the horoscopes of materialists, but simply using the astrological language for convenience, it should be easy to see how otherwise reputable thinkers are capable of such absurd reactions when commenting on parascience, or any form of occultism. In view of this we should all be able to relax and ignore these unfortunate outbursts. But can we? Don't we in fact find that, however much we explain them away, we still find the opinions of such people very irritating - dare I say even 'disturbing'? Why is this so?

THE OCCULTIST'S OWN SHADOW

Appropriately enough for lovers of symmetry, the answer lies in our own shadows. If you can allow me the same degree of oversimplification as before, I will illustrate in the same language.

Have you not observed how the mystical Piscean character of some occult groups can be a cover for an undercurrent of the lowest Virgoan critical backbiting? How the kingly Leonine Thelemite can sometimes show as a Mr Average, on the run from his own inferiority feeling of being 'just one of the crowd' (the lowest manifestation of Aquarian universality)? How the deep and dedicated penetration into life's mysteries bestowed by Scorpio so often results in a group which exploits those findings for the material gain of Taurus. Lastly there is the Sagittarian occult philosopher, searching for the unifying principles behind all phenomena thereby to win his freedom from them - does he not have at the back of his mind a Geminian cynic, quietly asking him whether there is any '*real* proof', quietly reminding him that perhaps his magic *is* only self deception?

It is towards this last problem that Johnstone's work was most particularly directed. He was happy to leave the 'born magicians' to get on with it. His concern was that the scientific world view had grown sterile and suffocating and that many people would be looking for a way out. In his mind the natural successor to a scientific world view was a magical world view (as is explained in the penultimate chapter of SSOTBME). The sort of thinking I have ascribed to the Sagittarian occultist would play a very important part in this transition. In which case we should expect the corresponding 'shadow' to be very active at the same time.

So will all 'born witches' get on with their spells, please; and I would like the rest of my readers to stop and to think.

Can you face up to the fact that, deep down inside you, there is a little part of you which does not really believe in magic? That suggests that the real reason you try to believe in magic is simply spite - because you hate the authoritarian, know-all smugness of the materialists? That points out that, although you love to listen to rumours of secret government research into parapsychology, vastly more research is actually being done into chemical and surgical techniques of character manipulation? That, for every step towards acceptance of parascience, computer science leaps forward a mile? That, despite what we like to believe about flying saucers, the bulk of government spending is on weapons of destruction rather than interstellar communication? Finally that suggests to you that, for all your raving about the Establishment's 'blindness', they could just be right after all? and soon they will have the necessary drugs or brain surgery to make you admit the fact?

Some of you will recognise the reality, the strength, of what I have suggested. Some will angrily deny it: of these there are some who will later come to admit what they dare not at first. Those who do not know this shadow are blessed, but they should look elsewhere for their own shadow, and not feel they do not have one!

THE WAY TO TRANSFORMATION

What is one supposed to do about the 'shadow'? By all accounts there comes a time in every progressive life when one is forced to accept it, or else miss the chance of further advancement. We fear to do so because we fear that 'acceptance of' means 'surrender to' - whereas acceptance should in theory lead to a transmutation.

One of Johnstone's pupils realised that he was engaging too much of his thinking life in imaginary arguments with a very dogmatic rationalist he had once crossed words with. In trying to see why he was so obsessed by thoughts of attacking these other beliefs, he came to recognise that the real enemy was in his own mind. Part of him did not believe in magic at all.

For many years he had been hoping to find a 'secret chief' or adept who would transform his life, and yet had always held back in his search. Suddenly he could see that fundamentally he had never believed in such wisdom: the history, if not the literature, of occultism was too full of accounts of those who had dedicated their lives to the search for a master, and had ended up at the feet of some egotistical junky.

Walking alone one fine day he dared to ask himself what *did* he really believe? Swiftly came the answer that 'magic was bunk' and the 'rationalists were right'. Fortunately he resisted the temptation just to smack himself and forget this lapse. Instead he examined the answer more closely.

True, he did not really believe in the Wisdom of the ancients, nor in the Geller phenomenon, the Loch Ness Monster or flying saucers ... And so it went on, all the barricade of beliefs he had sheltered behind was crumbling away until he came to the point where something real remained.

He realised that he *did* believe that the universe was slightly more 'connected up' than the materialists would allow. For example, his horoscope told him recognisable things about himself. Although they were rather woolly statements, they were less woolly than the rationalists' attempts to explain away the coincidence as a 'form of self deception'.

This was his shadow's weak point then - his world was rather more 'connected' than materialist theory would allow. Realising this fact freed him, and he was able to construct his own magical theory based upon that fact. Thus he gave up tilting at windmills and came in his turn to sit at the feet of an egotistical old junky. Music please...

JOHNSTONE'S PATH

Here is one individual solution to one individual problem. What we want to do is to explore more general techniques for transmuting our own inner fears and doubts.

As the alchemical process begins with the black state, and the ascent of the middle pillar begins with the path of Saturn, as does Jung's path to liberation begin with the recognition of the shadow, so does Johnstone's method so often begin by assuming the most objectionably mechanistic world view, and proceeding to deduce wonders from it. In particular we are now concerned with the example that I wrote about in the last issue of *Arrow* which says that if reality is mechanistic and so able to be duplicated by a sophisticated machine, then the chances are that we and our whole apparent universe are in fact just such a model, that we are in fact living in a dream within some giant computer.

LIVEABLE REALITIES

Is this idea of the world a 'liveable reality'?

Johnstone called a world view a 'liveable reality' if, once you started to believe it, it began to prove itself true. Livable realities need not be nice, or even sensible to outsiders: obviously the materialist world view was liveable, as was the view held by some that all the troubles of the world were caused by Jews.

I believe the answer is 'yes'. If you begin to believe in the computer model of the brain, you begin to find a lot of evidence for it, and you find that the advance of computer science is gradually eroding man's uniqueness. (The fact that, if you *don't* believe the model, you find the advance of computer science equals an advance of administerial bungling is quite beside the point.)

Apart from this outside evidence there comes an inner, philosophical confirmation of the model. If we accept it, we find that we can begin to reconcile what was seen as the most arrogant materialist assumption with certain very ancient mystical teachings. For example, if the whole universe is a dream being worked out within a computer then the ancient view that matter is 'maya' or illusion can be reconciled with the fact that it seems so real to us, who are also parts of that dream. Secondly this model confirms the mystical view of the one-ness of the universe: whereas it is hard to see how the disjoint 'real' materialist universe can be reconciled with astrology, or apparent action at a distance, all this becomes credible if we are all part of one transcendent machine. Thirdly the model gives us an image of how there can be a creator of this universe, and how that creator can live outside time and space as we know it.

THE HONEYMOON

If you allow yourself to live within this reality for a while it begins to show many such advantages. So many traditional beliefs about the world, that previously one hardly dared to believe in, suddenly become possible. What at first sight seems to be a rather cramped and sterile world view gradually unfolds to reveal a world much larger and more mysterious than ever seemed possible before. As was explained in the last article, the less magic that exists in the meta-reality, the more likely that magic will have been programmed into our reality.

What is more, this belief bestows greater dignity and power upon the individual, and this is highly desirable in an age where the bureaucracy of the super state is threatening to crush us all. How does it bestow that dignity? If my individual consciousness is part of one vast machine that includes the whole universe, then it means that it is ultimately possible for introspection to reveal as much about the universe as a multi-billion pound government research project. The way inward is as powerful as the way outward. As above, so below.

These examples illustrate that this world view has certain advantages. If it were generally accepted there would be a renewed sense of awe and mystery, a readjustment between the known and the un-known. Having recognised the advantages let us now explore the idea a little.

EXPLORING THE MODEL

It is typical of human curiosity to begin by wondering who or what created this world, and what resemblance has it to that creator's own universe? Here I have presented a world model which opens up a vista of new possibilities, and we immediately turn our back on these gifts and ask questions about the meta-universe beyond.

At first we can say nothing of the meta-universe, except that it was capable of conceiving this universe. All our physical laws might be arbitrary constructs of some artistic crank. It would be unwise to assume that the meta-world is composed of the same elements as ours appear to be, and that the computer in which we exist is necessarily made of silicon chips. However, it is perhaps not unreasonable to assume that certain fundamental principles might still apply: for example the principle of economy in nature. The computer may not be made of silicon chips, but it is likely to try to make best use of its capabilities.

One way to economise would be to cut back on redundant phenomena. Perhaps as you read this you hear a drip on the window pane which tells you that it is beginning to rain. Unless you look up at the pane that drip will only have registered as a sound in your consciousness. If we assume that drop of rain had objective existence then that one drop is made up of an enormous amount of information. A scientist with time to waste could make a lifetime's study of its formation, trajectory, the impact on the pane, the physical properties of the liquid and the constituent particles etc. Yet its only impact on your consciousness was to make a sound which tells you it is raining. So it would be an obvious economy to do without the 'actual' raindrop and simply reproduce the impact of its noise on your consciousness. There are assumed to be many more drops of rain falling on your roof - but unless they are going to be noticed why give them 'real' existence in the model?

This is the version of reality which says that the tree in the courtyard does not exist unless someone is perceiving it. Instead of running the whole universe in your model you only run the phenomena which are due to impinge upon consciousness at some time. But in the example of the tree, how does the tree cease to exist when you look away from it? It needs to be kept in store for later perceptions, so it might just as well continue to 'exist'. Did the far side of the moon exist before the spacemen went there? It need not have done, but, as it eventually needed to be created, perhaps it was planned in advance and kept in store to give consistency to the model.

Returning to our drip on the pane, how does the machine calculate how to make exactly the right noise at the right time? If this is to be done for every drop that is to be perceived, perhaps (for reasons given the next paragraph) it is in the long run simplest to model the whole event of the raincloud, even when only a tiny part of the model is going to impinge on consciousness. As this modelling is what we mean by 'existence', this would suggest that perhaps the whole cloud *does* exist as a mathematical formula even if we only perceive one drop which needs to be calculated from it.

Another way of economising would be to cut back on the number of independent parameters in the universe. If every molecule has its own independent existence, if every created being is an island, then the amount of information stored is staggeringly huge. But what if the universe was instead built out of permutations of a limited number of factors, as described in the essays on the I Ching (for example Ta Chuan in Book II of the Wilhelm version). Then it could happen that all simultaneous events, being based on permutations of a smaller set, would be linked, despite their spatial separation. In this case it could begin to make sense to judge a person's make-up by the position of the stars at their birth, or, when a problem is present in your mind, to seek a solution to it in the 'chance' layout of tarot cards, of yarrow stalks, of planetary positions or any other oracle. In such a world phenomena like telepathy or dowsing become possible without any need for any perceptible means of transmission of information. The whole notion of 'coincidence' takes on a different meaning in this model.

Another economy would be to avoid completely scrapping souls at death, by refurbishing them for re-use. In other words to programme re-incarnation into the universe.

An interesting thing about the above arguments is that the principle of economy in nature is the very one which so often inspires scientists to reject occult phenomena - eg: "If our model adequately describes human behaviour without invoking the idea of a 'soul', then there is no soul". But in this case we find the principle of economy being applied to the number of independent variables in nature suggests the likelihood of a whole range of 'unacceptable' occult phenomena! The reason why the fact has not been more obviously apparent is suggested in *Thundersqueak*, and in an article on 'Parascience' in an earlier issue of *Arrow*.

We cannot make any certain assumptions about the meta-universe, but if we tentatively assume that the principle of economy applies then we can make some suggestions about the nature of this universe. Some of these will not be possible to verify without gaining access to the original 'program', others might prove verifiable by experiment.

FREE WILL

Another question that springs to mind is the question of free will. Does this computer model of the universe deny free will? Are all our actions utterly determined by the automatic working out of the initial conditions (including of course the built in illusion that our will is free)?

Again we will have to make some 'wild' assumptions about the meta-universe when we ask why this one was created. If this universe has been created let us continue to assume it was 'deliberately' created, in which case it can be assumed to have some sort of 'value'. We then ask what could be the value of creating an utterly deterministic universe in comparison with a non-deterministic universe? The former might be created with one particular 'end' in view - in other words a universe created to calculate a solution to one particular problem. But, looking at the complexity of existence, one cannot help but feel that the means are over-elaborate to justify such an end.

So, if we are bold enough to assume any sense of 'art' exists in the meta-universe, then it seems likely that life is not utterly pre-determined, for a non-deterministic universe is so much more valuable.

So how much freedom is there? Anyone who chooses to observe soon realises just how much apparent free will is in fact not free - just how stereotyped much of our lives can be. But what is here being questioned is those occasions when a decision is made in full consciousness - how true is our apparent freedom of choice in such cases?

The difficulty is to imagine how one could build freedom into the system. One solution is suggested near the end of this essay, but until then we will satisfy ourselves by seeing how *little* freedom we need to build it.

Let us say I feel hungry. In this case I might eat a chocolate biscuit that is handy. Or else I might think ahead and not eat it because I am planning to have a slap-up lunch in half an hour. Or else I might go further and eat it, in order to save having to spend so much on lunch. Or I might not eat at all until the next day as a gesture towards third world starvation, or as a cleansing fast. My consciousness can operate on any decision at many different levels. Perhaps at every level the correct decision is utterly determined, but freedom consists simply of a freedom to move from level to level, and expansion of consciousness means an expansion of one's thinking to embrace more levels - and so win greater freedom.

What is suggested is that a universe with some degree of freedom built-in would be more 'valuable' or 'interesting' than a totally deterministic universe and so more likely to be created.

DIVINE INTERVENTION

A universe which allowed freedom might be more worthwhile, but it would also need much more careful adjustment. Indeed it would be very difficult to adjust it at all from 'outside'.

Let us imagine that 'god' never meant us to find out about nuclear power so soon, what can he do about it now? The obvious answer is to re-program the laws of physics to annul nuclear reactions - but that would produce catastrophic changes at every level of existence. Destroying all nuclear establishments would quite likely panic the politicians into another war ... and so on. The only way of predicting the outcome of any change from outside would be to do a computer run, and as the universe *is* the computer this is rather pointless. In the case of a non-deterministic universe it is especially pointless, because two runs on the same input might lead to different outcomes.

Any changes made in a non-deterministic universe will involve a lot of risk. The safest course is not to make clumsy changes from outside, but to enter into the universe itself in order to make the change. Only by becoming a human and accepting the limitations of a human existence could the creator hope to fully appreciate what changes are needed, and only as a human, working within the system, can changes of sufficient subtlety be brought about - even if one might be crucified in the process.

One snag is that the more of the godlike consciousness is carried into the body, the less easy it is to totally enter the human condition. So, possibly, subsequent world teachers have attempted to direct the course of history with only a comparatively hazy realisation of their true status. For instance they might see themselves as beings from another star system, or as humans 'possessed' by a god. Or even just perceptive thinkers. This model sheds new light on World Teachers and Sons of God.

A BIGGER, OR A SMALLER WORLD?

Those were just a few examples to show that we can still speculate about the nature of the universe even though we know nothing of the meta-world in which it was created. These examples should have given some idea of how open the possibilities are.

Earlier I suggested how a belief in this model could benefit society by widening our horizons, how then does it benefit the individual? We have transformed the apparently most constricting and sterile theory of materialist science - that of man as a machine - by extending it to its logical conclusion, and we have found that conclusion to be full of magic. By this means we have transformed the twentieth century occultist's 'shadow' and got it to co-operate with us. The findings of science are seen as part of a huge game, and are no longer seen as attacks on cherished beliefs. 'Flowers now grow in the dust', as Johnstone would say.

The computer model of the universe need only limit us if we kid ourselves that the present day computers represent the ultimate possibility. In fact whoever, or whatever, built this universe must have had abilities far beyond our present abilities - so who knows what undiscovered possibilities have also been created in our universe? This suggests a possible route towards the discovery of our True Will: the elimination of all that is automatic or mechanical in our nature. As each advance in machine intelligence is made the initiate would, in his meditation, discount the corresponding faculties in his mind and look towards what remains. Step by step he could approach that transcendent core of his being that must contain, or be, his True Will.

The possibilities are wide open, but all the same some readers may have read this far and still feel cheated by this world model, because they feel that I have replaced a mysterious transcendent Creator by some nasty know-all egghead scientist in a white coat who has constructed our universe within a computer just for a cold-blooded experiment? Then stop! Whoever suggested a 'nasty know-all scientist' as the Creator? That figure came out of your own mind: he is the very shadow we set out to overcome and he is trying to sabotage our efforts by getting back to the controls. You are tempted to reject this model because the shadow has taken up residence within it.

OLD WINE...

Myself I do not see this model in these terms, and here is why. Rudolf Steiner in his book *Occult Science* gives a long and tedious chapter on the evolution of the universe - not evolution since the 'big bang' but evolution before there was even any material existence. At great length he describes four levels of creation - the Saturn, Sun, Moon and Earth stages. Only the last one comprises matter, the Moon stage is rarified - a little like the dream world - and the Sun and Saturn stages are correspondingly even less corporeal. At each stage the universe is born, goes through an entire evolutionary cycle until it reaches its ultimate expression before being re-born at the next stage.

The only thing that kept me going through this detailed and tedious account was the recognition that it parallelled the cabalistic account of creation where the entire creation process of the Tree of Life is repeated in four worlds - the Malkuth or 'fruit' of each world becoming the Kether, or 'seed' of the next world. At each of the four levels the Tree is descended as far as Yesod, then we are told comes the 'fall', a change of state which sets an abyss between Yesod and Malkuth.

Knowing how dull such Kosmic Speculation can be I will present only a very brief summary of the process, skipping the detailed justification of the model as it will be familiar to many readers.

...IN NEW BOTTLES

I begin by skipping the description of the birth of manifestation from out of the Unmanifest. This is dealt with in Crowley's article *Berashith.* Sufficeth to say that from out of the Unmanifest came the seed of manifestation. From this seed grew a world or universe called Atziluth. This world is usually called the world of 'archetypes' or 'gods' but, as it contains nothing even as definite (or limited) as an abstract idea, I will simply call it a World of Possibilities.

This world was not created as a completed entity; only 'Kether', the initial seed, was created. From that seed evolved the world in ten stages symbolised by the ten sephiroth of the Tree of Life - with which I assume the reader is familiar.

According to tradition this evolution followed a regular course as far as the ninth sephirah. But at that point came a crisis. The creation of the tenth sephirah is described as a 'fall' - the creation of a whole new order of reality. This fall is as catastrophic a step as the original creation of Kether from the Unmanifest. This tenth sephirah is now the seed, or Kether of the next world which is called Briah, the World of Archangels or the World of Ideas. The World of Possibilities has given birth to the Possibility of an Idea.

The archetypal pattern having been set in Atziluth, we find that this new World of Ideas evolves from its own formless chaotic seed into a fully developed world in ten stages which echo the ten evolutionary stages of the previous world. So we find the Tree of Life repeated in Briah, and again the final stage is a 'fall' to a new order of existence. From Briah is born Yetzirah - the World of Images. With the birth of Malkuth in Briah we find that the World of Ideas has given birth to the Idea of an Image. This Idea of an Image is the formless chaotic seed from which the World of Images evolves - a world we might describe as a 'dream world'.

Once again there are ten stages and a fall. The Tree of Life is repeated in Yetzirah. When Malkuth is created out of Yetzirah it marks the creation of a new order of existence, namely 'matter'. Created as formless chaos, being initially just the Image of Matter, this matter evolves and our universe is created in ten stages. It is only this last cycle of evolution which has been acknowledged and studied by contemporary science. Bearing this in mind, and the enormous timescale involved, we can look back on the earlier three worlds and get a better feeling for the immensity of each stage. Each of the previous three stages marks the complete development of a complete universe - not just a three-day 'tooling-up' job of a creator whose real aim was to make our present reality. It is this immense pre-creation which Steiner so wordily described as seen by his own spiritual vision.

This then is the traditional cabalistic story of creation. As such it is probably familiar to most readers. What we want to do now is to feel our way towards a better *understanding* of this creation. Why should a new order of reality be created? By what sort of method might it be possible to create the 'solid' world of matter from out of the 'insubstantial' world of dream?

To answer these questions let us come back to our present situation. On the vast timescales we have been considering we can say we now live in a 'complete' world. From formless chaos the World of Matter has evolved a structure, and that structure is sophisticated enough (in the form of Man) to examine the World of Matter itself. So this world is 'complete' on the cosmic timescale, even if it is not 'perfect' or 'exhausted' on our own timescale. Within this complete universe there are now beings (certain computer scientists) who claim that we are approaching the possibility of re-modelling our very physical existence in the form of binary computer logic.

In view of the many stupid things said in the name of science we must not be too quick to accept this claim. But consider, for example, digital sound reproduction. Music is often considered the most spiritual of the arts, music has been seen as the very foundation of our existence, but now music has been reproduced in digital form. What is more this reproduction is not a shoddy third rate reproduction - instead it is now setting a new standard of quality that surpasses earlier techniques. Though taking second place to live music, it has at least attained that second place in a very short time. One can begin to respect those scientists' claims in the light of what they have achieved so far. If music can be coded into binary logic perhaps consciousness can too.

In that case the time could come when this World of Matter will be capable of creating a new world, a whole new order of reality. Within a 'computer' of hitherto undreamed-of vastness a set of laws governing a new submaterial world could be programmed and the initial cloud of sub-matter 'created'. The World of Matter will have given birth to a whole new order of existence. When beings have evolved within that new universe they will be only able to speculate about our World of Matter which to them will be 'beyond time and space' - a veritable Dream World. But to us their dreams will be a concrete reality - the flow of electrons in the circuit of a computer.

When particle physicists look closely at the structure of our existence they get back beyond rock hard matter to reveal entities which are no more substantial than images to us. So could the creation suggested above not be a model for the creation of our own world of matter? Might not the images or Angels of Yetzirah have discovered the structure of their own level of reality, and have assembled that knowledge, that logic, to create a universe of matter? To their 'outsiders' eyes they were merely constructing an Image of Matter, to us it is a reality. Might not the Archangels or Ideas of Briah have structured the logic of their own level of existence to create the Image World of the Angels? And so on?

Do we now begin to have an understanding of the 'how' of creation? Such a fact of creation would well justify the gap between the tenth sephirah and the other nine, being a true 'fall' to a new order of existence. The structure, or relationships between entities on one world (rather than those entities themselves) forming the 'matter' of the next world, just as the relationships between transistors rather than the transistors themselves form the 'matter' of robot consciousness.

What then about the why of creation? In *Thundersqueak* there is a discussion of a short story in which such an act of creation takes place as the ultimate solution to a population crisis. The limitations of the physical universe were too great for the human masses to be transported to other habitable planets, instead a series of parallel universes were created within a computer and the peoples' consciousness was programmed into those new realities.

In the story those new worlds were created and modelled into a 'completed' form. To do so would have involved an appalling amount of preliminary calculation - every grain of sand and every blade of grass in every planet in every world would have had to be pre-calculated. To do so would have required a computer just as big as the final 'mother' computer. For this reason I suggest that it would be more realistic to follow the course I have here described - to merely input the initial conditions and to permit the universe to evolve itself. In that case the myriad human souls would each be put into memory store, or 'limbo' until the universe had evolved an appropriate body for each to inhabit. Our model begins to sound even closer to that described by Steiner!

This idea of each universe being a 'working out' or evolution from an initial set of conditions provides a possible mechanism for Johnstone's Law of General Psychic Relativity which is discussed in *Thundersqueak*. Briefly stated this law says that the inertia of any region of the universe is a function of *all* the conscious beliefs in that universe.

For example, this law would explain why the incidence of miracles increases as we go back in history to times when there was less scepticism about miracles. It would also explain the fact that the most striking modern psychic phenomena seem to occur at odd moments when there are few witnesses - ie in a restricted universe containing fewer sceptical minds - and that they lose their credibility when later published. (The accepted explanations for these two facts are that a) people were sillier in the past and b) lonely people are either silly or liars). In this model the ancient world was less 'worked out' - for example human consciousness had not yet crystallised the laws of physics - and so there was more room for miracles in the correspondingly looser structure. The world picture is like the creation of a pen and ink drawing, the fine cross hatching and shading is still being slowly filled in. In ancient times when only the main outlines were complete there was more freedom to alter the picture. Now the picture is more detailed and so less flexible, there was not room enough for Uri Geller to overthrow the scientific status quo. The fact that we can still witness miracles if, for example, we go alone into the wilderness and keep our mouths shut, is because it is possible to ignore the whole picture and focus on your own private corner of it. When viewed in close up we can see the spaces between the lines and there is still room to make changes.

Does this mean then that the age of magic is over? No, not if we are prepared to change the picture rather than to squeeze new details into the one that science has given us. If everyone started to believe in the model I am now describing we might all be riding around on non-polluting broomsticks in a century or two!

Overpopulation - one reason to create a new reality. Another more interesting reason will be considered in the next paragraph, but first I would like to draw attention to an intriguing idea that the last model has suggested. It is the idea that beings from the previous order of reality could somehow come to populate the new level - to enter as 'souls' into the new 'bodies'. In this case the previous reality would partake in, and have an interest in the new reality of a quite different order to the 'artistic' curiosity which we considered earlier and in the last article.

Why should a dream world create a world of matter in this way? If Yetzirah is as we picture it with the freedoms of a dream world, why should the 'angels' choose to enter into the limitations of physical existence, to put on the burden of a material body? Perhaps the following analogy will suggest a possible reason.

Imagine that the present evolution of mankind had taken a slightly different course, without attaining our own mastery of mobility. A civilisation of what we would consider to be 'cripples' had evolved and provided some very wise men. Such was their wisdom that certain of them began to feel their limitations. They realised that something else was needed before they could extend their mastery, and that something was 'mobility'. For the sake of consistency I should now say that they created machines for transport; however, the idea of machine consciousness is still not easy to grasp so instead I will assist the imagination by saying that these wise men turned to the wild creatures and, by selective breeding, created horses. Having created this 'new reality' they had to learn to mount and ride these horses. This was not easy. For the horses had evolved a consciousness of their own and could put up considerable resistance. The situation was even more difficult because there were also plenty of less wise men who were eager to grab the reins themselves - or even to sabotage the scheme by distracting and panicking the horses in an attempt to dislodge their rightful riders. But those few horses that learned to ignore these distractions, to overcome them and to gain rapport with their riders, were able to achieve a new freedom. Horse and rider together became one greater entity, with new power to rule the land and bring order to the world.

Could this story suggest another type of relationship between the World of Images and the World of Matter: that the angels needed to cloak themselves in matter in order to complete their work? In this case we are their vehicles, buffeted by demons and doubts and blinkered by our own sense of identity. Until we each find our True Will and join forces with our Holy Guardian Angel, we will never find that true freedom.

In this model we find that our physical existence - albeit an 'illusion' and a 'limitation' - is something that is prized by the angelic beings. As is suggested in Jung's *VII Sermones Ad Mortuos* 'numberless gods await the human state' or 'the gods are many, whilst men are few'. The struggles and obsessions described in *Thundersqueak* are the lower demons of Yetzirah scrabbling to incarnate by gaining a foothold in our souls.

An article in *New Scientist* in the 70s suggested that soon Science might come to know everything. Truly the details are too numerous for anyone's knowledge: what was suggested was that we might be approaching the position of knowing all the basic laws of existence. The ability to create a new universe in the way I have suggested would be tantamount to having that knowledge. What then of our religious feelings? How small and frustrating our vaster universe would seem to those most advanced thinkers who first reached that understanding!

Here is a different sort of 'overpopulation': minds who have grown too big for the material world, rather than bodies who have grown too numerous. To have that knowledge and yet to have failed to create the perfect society - that is the direction in which we are progressing. Like the wise men we pictured on the angelic plane might not our leading thinkers feel compelled to create a new reality in order to extend the battle onto new territory - to widen their horizons into a whole new order of reality?

Actually I am not really engaged in making predictions at this point, although it might read like it. What I am asking is 'can we see possibilities in our present condition which will help us to understand what might have happened before? Does this throw light on the 'why' of creation?

As to the future there is a major doubt. Although it seems very reasonable for creation to continue ever downwards, a substantial body of tradition claims that this material universe in fact marks a lowest point of evolution and that the future holds an involution back towards godhead. Could this idea simply be a reflection of inadequate imagination on the part of previous generations? being unable to imagine anything more 'solid' than matter and not understanding the true nature of the creative process, did they therefore just assume that the end had been reached? I feel that this was not so. The cabalistic model shows so great an understanding of the process that it is most reasonable to accept that it was based on knowledge that had been input from the 'higher' worlds.

Therefore I am inclined to trust the assertion that the future lies towards the spiritual rather than down towards a new creation. After all, the discovery of atomic fusion amounts to a discovery of how to erase certain files in the computer memory. The knowledge that we are gaining as to how we could create a new universe is not a red herring so long as that knowledge opens our eyes to the true nature of our own existence. For then the ascent can begin in earnest, only the first stage of which is the return to one-ness with our angelic nature.

For what happens when we attain unity with the guardian angel? It is just the first step, for that 'angelic' world must itself be mastered. But can that happen until the angel has realised its own oneness with its own inner archangel - for whom and by whom the world of angels was created? And beyond that lies the Kingdom of gods before we once more can merge with the unmanifest, according to our cabalistic model. In this model we are already half way through evolution - but it is an evolution that is seven times bigger than the evolution now recognised by science. According to this traditional view, then, our forthcoming development of computer technology is not destined to lead evolution down along an endless chain of realities. Instead it will be the key to the understanding of our own evolution, from whence we can begin the ascent back to godhead.

CONCLUSION

We have ended up right back at the traditional cabalistic world view, with the four worlds and each human with his own 'guardian angel', and higher bodies. Self cultivation, or finding one's True Will consists of turning away from the hubbub of obsessions around us, which are trying to possess us. Only when local thoughts in the machine are quelled does there come awareness of the higher nature, and the path to initiation commences.

So what have we achieved? Our new approach has got us nowhere. But that is what is so interesting.

At the beginning of this essay I addressed myself to those of us who would have liked to embrace a traditional model of man's make-up, but who found that, whenever they faced it, a nagging voice of doubt was always heard over their shoulder. So what we did was call that Doubt's bluff. We turned round and set off in the opposite direction towards the idea of man as machine. At the end of our journey we were back where we started. It appears that the universe of belief must be closed, finite and curved as is the universe of matter - just as would be expected in our model!

Our argument has got us where we wanted. It has got us nowhere. Nowhere is the beginning of all possibilities.

Go out and look at the world. As you do so try to live this new model of reality - feel your thoughts and perceptions as processes in the vast machine of a unified universe. The world becomes fresh and full of a new mystery and potential. We witness the re-birth of Reality.

But is it *true?* Johnstone never explained any particular model in terms of its truth, but only in terms of its ability to foster this re-birth and give joy, hope and freedom. Philosophy with the emphasis on 'philo' instead of 'sophy'. Surely the appropriate approach for the Age of Horus?

As was promised in the first section I have tried to present the idea in a form that is helpful to the individual. The fact that, along the way, I have laid the foundation of a whole new philosophy of existence, a world religion that (for once) actually depends upon the co-operation of scientific advance, is, I am sure, just the sort of good value that my readers have learnt to expect!

ANALOGUE

A mighty King ruled the land. As a young man he had appeared as a saviour to the people, defeating the tyrant that oppressed them and bringing new freedom and hope. Now the people were prosperous and well fed thanks to the King's wise policies. Yet they were not content. Around the city the King had built mighty fortifications to protect his realm, but now the people felt cramped by these walls, choked in the confines of their own prosperity.

Hearing the people's cries of complaint, young warriors had come from other lands to challenge the Kingship, but the mighty walls kept them at bay. The King grew older, and harder on these claimants.

One day the King's valet announced the presence of a new challenger to the throne.

"I have nothing to fear!" the old King bellowed, "Have not my walls already repulsed Spiritualism, Theosophy, UFOs, Gurdfieff, Geller and the Psychedelic invaders from the East? No-one will take my throne from me!"

"But Sire," answered his valet, "this challenger comes not from without..."

At this a callow youth burst into the room, awkwardly wielding a sword.

"I am the challenger!" he cried.

The King stepped back alarmed, angry. Restraining his wrath he quietly but firmly spoke.

"You cannot kill me, for I am your own father!"

"You are not my father," said the youth. "For my father was an idealistic and vigorous warrior who defeated the tyrant Religion in single combat. Whereas you are yourself an old and hidebound tyrant who hides behind fortifications and ignores his people's changing needs.''

Whereupon the King drew his sword and spoke again.

''How dare you, a mere stripling, challenge a mighty warrior who has fought and conquered to build this reality. For that you will die a traitor.''

The youth bit his lip nervously but spoke firmly.

''Remember only that you have not faced a challenger on equal terms for over one hundred years, whereas I have been practising daily for this challenge.''

The two stood facing each other in silence.

The youth farted nervously.

3 - THE ANTS IN THE PANTS OF THE DANCING WU LI MASTERS...

First Published in Arrow 10

The third Johnstone's Paradox article (don't give up, the next one in this book is about something else). Sorry about the rather flip introduction - I was parodying the way certain columnists in the New Scientist used to write (can't think why).

As mentioned, I was trying to give up writing at the time. Pluto was opposing my Sun, so I was actually trying to give up almost everything.

INTRODUCTION

Having emptied the contents of my brain onto the pages of Arrow in the form of two concluding articles on 'Johnstone's Paradox' I had decided that Ramsey Dukes' literary days were done and it was time to concentrate on weightier matters such as copulation and the size of my bank balance. Last year I celebrated this bold decision by buying *The Tao of Physics* to read - and later *The Dancing Wu Li Masters.*

It was while reading the latter that I came upon the passage about 'Bell's Theorem' quoted below, whereupon my nostrils flared and flecks of foam appeared upon my lips. Little did I then realise that, from that moment, Arrow readers were doomed to another article from my pen.

(Theorem One: when a regular contributor to a magazine starts writing much about her\himself, it is indeed time she\he stopped writing).

As it was the more recent of the two volumes to fall drained of wisdom from my sweaty grasp, I will concentrate my attention on the Dancing Wu Li Masters.

This book describes physicists' attempts to discover the fundamental units of existence, since the time when it was discovered that what were presumptuously called 'atoms' turned out not to be fundamental after all. It describes the newest candidates - the fundamental particles - and their very peculiar behaviour. In particular it describes the bizarre conclusions that have been drawn from their behaviour - 'conclusions' is too strong a word, 'confusions' is a little closer.

What physicists wanted was to find the basic 'Leggo' bricks from which all matter could be built. Having discovered that colliding particles tend to reform into different particles as if they were in fact complex bodies, they wondered whether any truly fundamental particles could be identified from which the others could be constructed. In fact it seems that particles can under different circumstances divide and reform in a whole lot of ways. It is beginning to seem that a particle is not so much a solid object as a collection of possibilities. It is even said that, even when not colliding, a particle is constantly splitting and re-forming in a dance of 'virtual particles' ('virtual' because they break and re-form too quickly for observation or measurement).

If the simplest units of matter are so very immaterial, what about our conceptions of time and space? We talk of a particle being generated at one point, A, accelerated in a certain direction and then colliding or otherwise reacting at another point, B. Is it really the same particle that moves from A to B? Our intuition that this is so is supported by various observations. Firstly the particle seems to obey the laws of motion between A and B, secondly if we cause it to pass through photographic emulsion we find a definite trail marking the particle's passage. However these 'laws of motion' are a pre-existing assumption in our thinking, and that is dangerous in an area of study where the observations we make appear to be profoundly affected by the way we make them (and so by the assumptions upon which we base our search).

In the case of the photographic emulsion, if we look at it too closely the solid trail breaks into a series of dots, where individual molecules of the sensitive material have been activated. Instead of a continuous locus through space we have a string of billions of separate particle detectors, all registering positively. Physicists no longer feel confident in claiming that from this we can reach any conclusion about the motion of the particle *between* each molecule; all they can admit is that at some point in the given time interval a particle was present at each of the points in question.

To cut a long story short we come to Bell's Theorem. Having found evidence that there is apparently an instantaneous transfer of information between separate localities (a particle at one point seems to know what is happening elsewhere) this suggests several possibilities. 1) a totally predetermined universe (whatever the experimenter thinks he is doing in fact the outcome was decided before he even started). This unpopular idea was suggested, and I hope argued out of, as a possible deduction from Johnstone's Paradox in the last article. 2) That something conveys information between the particles and it does so much faster than the speed of light. This idea is also unpopular. 3) That apparent separation in space-time is in fact an illusion. This rather 'Eastern' idea is too unfamiliar to the West to have had any chance of becoming popular. 4) Bell's Theorem suggests that the universe is in fact a whole, that apparently isolated objects and events are in fact linked within a fundamental structure that lies beyond our perception. This is the same conclusion that I deduced from Johnstone's Paradox in the previous articles. 5). There are other possibilities such as a 'many worlds' theory.

I do not intend to flaunt my ignorance of the subject by trying to expound further. Instead I will economise on literary effort by quoting several passages from the book itself.

THE QUOTES

Quote 1

'In 1964 J S Bell, a physicist at the European Organisation for Nuclear Research in Switzerland zeroed in on this strange connectedness in a manner that may make it the central focus of physics in the future.... Bell's Theorem was reworked and refined over the following ten years until it emerged in its present form..... One of the implications of Bell's Theorem is that, at a deep and fundamental level, the 'separate parts' of the universe are connected in an intimate and immediate way. In short, Bell's Theorem and the enlightened experience of unity are very compatible.'

('Bell's' Theorem indeed! Why not 'Dukes' Theorem? Sure I said it six years after Bell but, as the book points out, such time differences are merely a function of one's space-time perspective.)

Quote 2

'Thus one is led to a new notion of *unbroken wholeness* which denies the classic idea of analysability of the world into separately and independently existent parts.'

Quote 3

'According to Sarfatti's theory, the wave function of the photon pair is at a 'higher level of reality' than the wave functions of the separate photons ... In other words the whole is always greater than the sum of its parts.'

Quote 4

'In short the physical world, according to quantum mechanics is ... not a structure built out of independently existing unanalysable entities, but rather a web of relationships between elements whose meanings arise wholly from their relationship to the whole.'

(That the universe is an interconnected wholeness is tantamount to saying that the universe is one huge machine. In the last article I suggest this might be so, but the world as we see it is not the machine itself, but something of a different order of reality - in the same way that a calculation in a computer is of a different order of reality to the actual computer circuitry. In other words the linking mechanism behind phenomena lies not in the physical world but in a different ('higher') level of reality which we might as well call 'etheric' 'astral' 'spiritual' or whatever.

That was what I suggested. This book too suggests that the connection between particles exists outside physical reality. Does this not support my suggestion?)

Quote 5

"Reality" is what we take to be true. What we take to be true is what we believe. What we believe is based upon our perceptions. What we perceive depends upon what we look for. What we look for depends upon what we think. What we think depends upon what we perceive. What we perceive determines what we believe. What we believe determines what we take to be true. What we take to be true is our reality.'

(It is just as well Arrow has limited circulation - I've a nasty feeling I might owe the author some money for so much quoting. To make up for this travesty I will recommend you all to buy "The Dancing Wu Li Masters' to get the whole story.)

To sum up: I found in this book a strong case to support the ideas of my last article 'A New Muddle of the Oniverse'. To explain why is the purpose of this article. I present my case, as usual, in the form of an analogy (thus confirming that, unlike fundamental particles, I at least am predictable).

THE ANALOGY

For this analogy I am going to ask you to imagine that you have a sort of super Hewlett Packard programmable calculator, one so powerful that its internal processes have achieved the state of forming a conscious and coherent universe in the way that I have suggested might be possible in these articles.

But first I must make an apology. All through this series of articles I have told you *not* to make the assumption that the machinery of the universe is as crude as our present understanding of the word 'machine'. With our present state of development of, and attitude towards, computers I know that I can expect a negative reaction when I try to suggest that our universe might exist in the 'mind' of a mighty cosmic computer. So that you do not dismiss my thesis too hastily I have asked you to avoid this too obvious and crude picture of the clever computer. But now I am going against my word and asking you to fall back on just such a picture, because I believe that anyone who has understood the previous two articles will not by now fall into the trap of thinking 'Does this idiot really believe the universe is *nothing but* a super Hewlett Packard calculator!' (A True Master knows when to make, and break, his own rules. So what?)

Inside this calculator of yours is a universe, the 'objects' in this universe are 'really' (ie. to our outside eyes) just 'calculations'. The conscious beings or 'humans' in this universe are 'really' just very complex 'programmes'.

(We cannot go on with all these inverted commas, for the rest of this section I will write normally when writing in terms of the little universe inside your calculator but will write in italics when re-describing it as seen by us outsiders).

Some of these humans (*programs*) are scientists and they seek to discover the laws of their universe, in particular to find what matter (*calculations*) is made of. They have long speculated that it might be made of indivisible 'atoms'. In recent years they have actually managed to isolate these atoms (*numbers*) for the first time. All objects (*calculations*) in their world are in fact made of these atoms (*numbers*). However they have gone on to discover that atoms are not in fact indivisible, but they have a definite internal structure. They consist of an unchanging nucleus around which there lies a cloud of particles which fall into discrete orbits. *(In other words numbers (atoms) consist of an unchanging decimal point (nucleus) around which cluster digits (particles) in definite positions (orbits).* For example the atom 32.01 consists of a '3' particle (*digit*) in the 'tens' orbit, a '2' particle (*digit*) in the 'units' orbit, nothing in the 'tenths' orbit and a '1' particle in the 'hundredths' orbit.'

(*Notice already certain fundamental differences between this analogy and our universe: their 'atoms' are one dimensional, while ours are three dimensional; on the other hand they have particles orbiting both sides of the nucleus (inside and outside as it were). Or perhaps these inner particles should be called the nucleus and the decimal point seen as just a boundary?)*

A new breed of scientists - 'particle physicists'- have since made a lot of experiments with atoms. They have found, for example, that they can add energy to the atom 32.01 and make the 3 particle jump to other orbits to make 302.01, 3002.01 and so on. They have also matched the dreams of their ancient alchemists by breaking 32.01 down into different atoms such as 31+1.01, 30+2+.01 and so on. But having discovered that atoms are not the indivisible units of the universe they want to know what *is*. Obviously the 'particles' must be.

They have discovered ten particles 0,1,2,3,4,5,6,7,8 and 9 of which nine posses 'antiparticles' -1, -2, -3 to -9. Unfortunately these particles have proved not to be themselves indivisible - for example 9 can split into three 3s or 7+2, and so on. There was a flurry of excitement when one team in the Bloggsland Institute of Technology confirmed a theory that all particles can be made up of just three, namely -1, 0 and 1, but this hope was soon shattered when Finkstein in the same year broke a '1' into '3' and a '-2' (since then it has been split into a '7' and a '-6' and two '-4s' and a '9', and many other combinations).

It was after this last revolution that the 'new physics' was formulated. Scientists were forced to admit that these particles did not obey the laws of 'macroscopic' matter. For example any particle such as a '9' is really not so much a 'solid' material entity as a matrix of probabilities or 'virtual particles' (7+2, 3+3+3, etc etc in the case of a '9'). In fact there is a sense in which it can be said that any one particle includes *every* other one! Argument is still raging as to whether particles can even be ascribed individual existence - in what sense is a 9 in one atom different from a 9 in another atom, or are they both just two manifestations of a sort of '9 Field' that pervades all of reality?

(*Meanwhile, back in the real world we are falling about with laughter as we listen to these idiots trying to make experiments on digits as if they were billiard balls! Some of them seem to be getting towards the real point, however....*)

At a recent conference the new doubts were brilliantly outlined in Blenkinsop's paper. He raised the question as follows. When particle is moved through space (*ie 'rolled up the register' through a series of memory stores*) it is no longer valid to argue that it is a discrete physical entity actually following a one dimensional locus in space. All we can say is that in the progress of a '9' from, say, Register Rl to register R2 we know that a measuring instrument placed in any intermediate register will record a 9 during the interval of movement. A 9 will appear in Rl, in R2, in R3 and so on in turn, but it is no longer valid to say it is the 'same 9', or to speculate that it has any real existence in the unmeasured 'spaces' between registers. A 9 appears in Rl, then a 9 appears in R2 - this tells us nothing about the nature of what happens between Rl and R2 for 'between Rl and R2' is a concept with no measureable existence. Similarly when a 3 jumps to a different orbit in an atom, from 301 to 3001 say, then it is not meaningful to talk about its movement 'between the hundreds and thousands orbits' - those two orbits might exist, but the space between them has no real meaning.

(*The joke is growing stale, let's turn away from the scientists and listen to another group of loonies in this ridiculous universe. Let's listen to the so-called occultists, as represented by a certain nobleman called Duke Ramsey.*)

Duke Ramsey argues that the scientists are not looking in the right place, they are not looking at the *real* building blocks of the universe, but only its 'illusionary manifestations'! "Show us the real ones then!" jeer the scientists.

"I can't *show* you them for they are ... well ... you could call them 'gods', or 'angels' or 'ideas?..'' The scientists roar with laughter. "For example there is the Moon..."

"You mean *that*" laughs a scientist, pointing at the sky.

"No!... well, not exactly," (laughter) "I mean more the Principle of Femininity and Change. Then there is Kali, which is sort of the Principle of Destruction. Oh dear, I cannot *show* you any of these things because they don't have any physical existence, I can only *feel* them, and recognise their physical manifestations, as it were".

The scientists, tears of laughter on their faces, go back to their laboratories to see if a vast input of energy is capable of converting 9 into 9 million, as predicted by theory.

(Poor old Duke Ramsey - if only we could talk to him! We know exactly what he means by an 'idea' for, as outsiders, we can detect it as an electrical pulse in the circuits of the calculator - something with no 'physical reality' in his world of numbers and calculations. The 'principle' he is struggling to define as Kali is simply the pulse that clears a memory register and this 'destroys' its contents - ie something he can 'feel' as an element of his own being, something he can recognise at a vastly more complex macroscopic level, yet something none of his kind will ever directly know in what they call 'reality'. We would just love to 'teach those scientists a lesson' by pressing the 'All Clear' button that would destroy their entire world at a stroke. But what is the point? they would not be aware of what had happened!)

THE CONCLUSION

We must now abandon this phantasy, as tears of laughter have given way to tears of sorrow for poor Duke Ramsey and his frustrating debate with the scientists. Let us instead listen to his counterpart in our 'real' world - Ramsey Dukes.

I, Ramsey Dukes, say let us consider this reality to be the manifestation of non physical ('spiritual') principles. The nearest I can get to describing these principles is by using the word 'ideas' (in the past they were called 'Gods', 'angels' and so on). This is an ancient and well used view of reality, perhaps most precisely outlined in the Kabalistic model of the Tree of Life in the four worlds, as described in the previous article.

When scientists struggle to locate the basic particles of existence we hope they are having fun because we would like them to get *something* for their labours. When we set out to devise a symbolic, minrocosmic representation of the world (Tree of Life, Tarot, I Ching, Holy Cube or any personal private system) we are *actually* doing what the scientists are *trying* to do.

This is only true when we know what we are doing; if we merely study these subjects in the form of 'dead dogma' and in terrified awe of our sources, then we are doing rather less. By 'study' I mean more than just 'memorising'. I mean active meditational and observational research into the relationships between parts.

To take an example using the symbols of astrology:- When we operate at the level of Duality there are only two symbols, Sun and Moon. These are polar opposites, they have nothing in common. When, however, we operate at the level of '6' there are only 6 symbols forming three pairs (Moon-Saturn, Mercury-Jupiter, Venus-Mars). At this level the Sun is not included, far from being the 'opposite' of the Moon, the Moon is now the Sun's representative (this is seen at the '12' level of the rulerships of the zodiac signs when each symbol of the 6 splits into a 'positive' and a 'negative' except for 'Moon' which becomes 'Moon' and 'Sun' (Cancer and Leo). At this level the polar opposite of Moon is not Sun, but Saturn. What does this alteration in the status of the Moon tell us about the Principle of the Moon itself?

The answer to this question, or at least the further ideas prompted by this question, is as fundamental to our existence as the debate about the existence of quarks is meant to be. In that case why is so much more attention paid to the latter question?

The answer is that the technology of physics is at present better developed than the technology of magic. (*The government of Bloggsland has just put forward a hundred million pounds for the building of a more powerful particle accelerator - tell me, Arrow Readers, what did you do with your last hundred million pounds?)* If we can be so presumptious, so big headed and so insulting to our elders as to suggest that in this century it is only in the last decade that magical philosophy has begun to be accepted on the sort of scale where it could have any chance of growing to rival physics, and if we can recall how much time, money, energy and thought has gone into physics since the 'new physics' was created, then we can see how far there is to go in our own work.

No doubt there were occasions early in this century when

Einstein dreamed of exploding an atom bomb over his most dogmatic opponents; I too would love to levitate the Pentagon by chanting a mantra, now that I can see that the obvious theoretical barriers to this act have been dissolved.

To quote again from *The Dancing Wu Li Masters:*

'A powerful awareness lies dormant in these discoveries: an awareness of the hitherto-unsuspected powers of the mind to mold 'reality', rather than the other way round.'

But I am still caught in the web of maya: as long as I wish to confound the sceptics, it reveals that their opinions *matter* to me. So long as their opinions *matter* I am not completely free of them and so my 'reality' is still bound partially by their rules. Therefore I must continue upon the slow road: I must wait until the deductions from Johnstone's Paradox are generally accepted before I perform my 'miracles'. The technology must grow slowly alongside the theory.

Einstein's model gained acceptance because a) it fitted the facts, b) it could make predictions. In these essays I have tried to show how my ideas do fit the facts; when will the theory be sufficiently developed to make its own predictions? What sort of predictions can it make?

Recently I have read political comments to the effect that in recent years we have become obsessed with 'hard men', 'brute force', 'tough policies' etc. The last phase I recall was an obsession with 'thrill seekers' 'the love generation' and so on. What do I see in this apparently irrational progression? In astrological terms I see a progression from 'Venus' towards 'Mars'. What series of symbols has 'Venus' followed by 'Mars' and what is it that preceds the two? Answer: a 'Mercury' phase. Sure enough we had this in the form of an obsession with 'newness', 'novelty' and 'getting about'. What therefore can we predict for the future? Answer: an obsession with Jupiterian values. But how will this show? A return to expansion? A revival of sporting values? A religious revival?

Obviously there is work to be done!

POSTSCRIPT

A word to those who see in the 'new physics' a *denial* of my thesis, arguing that a 'world machine' implies a fully determined universe rather different from the crazy mystical universe of the Wu Li Masters.

The question of 'free will' requires a whole essay on its own, but I have at least touched upon it in my last article.

As for the curious unpredictable behaviour of particles under observation, I must fall back upon my analogy. As suggested earlier let us crudely assume a correspondence between physical locations and individual memory locations in the machine. In this case the 'programme' that makes up a so-called 'human' might well, in some of its working, encroach upon or make use of memory stores outside of the boundaries of its own 'physical body'. In other words in this world a 'human' might possess a 'non-physical aura'. In particular a concentration by a 'human' upon a particular locality might well extend the 'aura' into that locality. In this case the locality is an observation point for a 'particle' experiment. If the information that makes up the 'particle' is to share memory space with the observing 'human' programme, then it is hardly surprising that the observer should affect the observation.

In other words the apparent 'crazy mystical' nature of these particles is in fact a projection of our own 'crazy mystical' nature - it is our physical selves that are unreal. Is not the dilemma between the particle and wave theories not just a projection of Hadit and Nuit respectively?

The solution to the mysteries of the new physics lies within ourselves. Bleep.

4 - NOTES TOWARDS THE DEPLOYMENT OF THE HUNGARIAN MAGIC CUBE AS A SYSTEM OF DIVINATION

First published in Arrow 11

This is a bit different. I was employed as a technical writer for the first time, and it went to my head a bit. So I decided to write this in approved Ministry of Defence technical documentation format... more or less.

Two developments have occurred since writing this piece. One is that a 4x4x4 magic cube has been produced (see para 9.4) and I bought one but am not laughing. The other is that someone has written a booklet on the use of the cube for divination: I believe it is called "The Oracle of Light". I bought a copy, but cannot find it - nor can I remember what system it recommended.

1. WHAT IS REQUIRED FOR DIVINATION:

1.1 A permutable set containing not too many members (eg. the 78 tarot cards as upper bound?) nor too few (eg. the 8 trigrams which needed to be extended for the I Ching system).

1.2 The set should preferably be "structured" for easier assimilation by the human mind (eg. the relationships between the astrological symbols, the various attributions of the tarot cards etc.)

1.3 Ideally the members of the set should link with, or suggest, other traditional symbols - though this correspondence need not be exact.

2. WHAT CAN THE MAGIC CUBE OFFER?

2.1 It is a portable (note especially the midget key ring cubes now available) permutable set. The key ring cubes are smaller than the Rider Traveller's Tarot yet perfectly legible and easy to manipulate.

3. WHAT DOES THE MAGIC CUBE CONSIST OF?

3.1 A cube whose 6 faces are made up of 9 (3x3) coloured squares, 6 colours equally distributed.

3.2 A rotation of the faces produces an extremely large number of possible permutations of these coloured squares in a way that is not too predictable (so not liable to conscious "fiddling" of answers).

3.3 The permutations are not totally random, for example:

a) There can only be 6 white squares in all, however the cube is permuted. The same is true of the other colours.

b) The centre squares on each face do not move relatively to each other.

NOTE 1: The above means it can always be meaningful to talk about a "correct" orientation of the cube.

c) Certain other fixed relationships between adjoining squares on edges exist.

NOTE 2: The above limits on the permutability need not invalidate the system. On the contrary they could suggest a structure that is in itself meaningful cf. in astrology where a Sagittarius ascendant MUST indicate a Gemini seventh house cusp, and so on.

4. STRUCTURAL ANALYSIS - PART 1

4.1 6 faces and 6 colours. Is there any structure here?

4.2 Yes, the 6 faces form 3 opposing PAIRS, immediately suggesting 3 POLARITIES (+ and -).

4.3 So we have 3 spatial dimensions (up-down, left-right, front-back) and a positive and negative face in each dimension.

4.4 What does "3" offer? Alchemical "sulphur, salt & mercury" corresponding to the astrological "cardinal, fixed & mutable" perhaps? and to Steiner's 3 functions of "willing, feeling and thinking"?

4.5 Let us imagine the cube upright before us and allocate meaning to its 3 directions as follows:

Up, down = **WILL** (cf. the upright rod or phallic symbol of will)

Left, right= **THINKING** (cf. the "weighing up" motion of the balance)

Front, back= **FEELING** (cf. a reaching forward and a shrinking back towards yourself)

4.6 Polarise the triplicity as follows:-

Yin		**Yang**
Rest	**WILL**	Change
Attraction	**FEELING**	Repulsion
Synthesis	**THINKING**	Analysis

4.7 The 6 colours are white, brown, blue, yellow, red and green. Suggested attribution is as follows:-

Brown = Rest	Change = White
Green = Attraction	Repulsion = Red
Blue = Synthesis	Analysis = Yellow

4.8 What traditional link does this suggest? Answer: the 6 planets as polar pairs, eg.

Saturn, Brown, Rest - Change, White, the Moon

Venus, Green, Attraction - Repulsion, Red, Mars

Jupiter, Blue, Synthesis - Analysis, Yellow, Mercury

NOTE 3: These 6 symbols clearly LINK with the astrological planets but need not be congruent with them. For example the Moon in this scheme is the antithesis of Saturn and therefore represents both the luminaries. So the astrological association of Moon with Subconscious would not fit here. Such anomalies do not destroy a system, they merely give thought for meditation. For example the very dynamic trump card of The Chariot seems an odd attribution to Cancer as described in a popular sun-sign guide, but this does not negate the tarot.

5. PRACTICAL STEP - 1.

5.1 We find that cubes are coloured wrongly for our purposes. However the colours are self adhesive labels which may be removed and replaced.

5.2 Re-colour your cube as follows:-

Bottom = brown, Top = white
Left side = blue, Right side= yellow
Front (toward you) = green, Back (away from you)= red

HUMOROUS ASIDE 1: On completing this step I had a cube whose harmonious balance of colours was much more pleasing to Libran aesthetic sensibilities. However the labels had stretched and distorted on being pulled off, so the result was offensive to Virgoan aesthetic sensibilities.

6. PRACTICAL STEP - 2

6.1 Place your re-coloured cube the correct way up in front of you and acquaint yourself with it by meditation upon its polarities and relative positions.

6.2 FRONT: Green, Venus, Attraction, Feeling reaching toward you. This is the face that is truly yours, for it is the only one directly facing you. It is the "first impression". It is the closest face. If the cube speaks to you, here surely lies the answer.

6.3 BACK: Red, Mars, Repulsion, Feeling reaching away from you. The face that is not for you to see, but the face that others first see.

6.4 LEFT: Blue, Jupiter, Synthesis. Thinking as revealed when you move to the left, ie. right brain thoughts, non-verbal. If the cube is speaking to you then this face must be a message to the non-verbal half of the brain. The left represents the past.

6.5 RIGHT: Yellow, Mercury, Analysis. Thinking as revealed when you move to the right, ie. left brain verbal thought. Here the cube is speaking to your logical brain. The right represents the future.

6.6 UP: White, The Moon, Change. Upward motion of the Will. Aspiration, light. The crown of the cube, the higher nature is here spoken to.
6.7 DOWN: Brown, Saturn, Rest, inertia or resistance. Downward motion of the Will. Again, like BACK, a side you do not see, but here no-one sees it. Hidden unconscious factors.

7. STRUCTURAL ANALYSIS - 2
7.1 In para. 6 we noted that certain faces were hidden. Does this mean they should not be read in divination?
7.2 To answer this we must ask how the cube is viewed.
7.2.1 As an authority: In which case it stands before one and speaks, and we have no right to probe those areas it does not reveal to us.
7.2.2 As a microcosm: In which case we can pick it up and examine it as we see fit. Here the diviner is active.
7.3 The difference surely lies in the style of the question as follows:-
7.3.1 Cube positive, diviner negative. A question of the form "Please advise me..." or "should I do this..." where we approach the cube as an authority.
7.3.2 Cube negative, diviner positive. A question of the form "What would happen if I..." or "Who will be victorious..." where the cube is expected to encapsulate a situation which will then be studied from all angles by the diviner.

8. PRACTICAL STEP - 3
8.1 Set up the cube before you again and continue the meditation in the light of the above.
8.2 In particular explore the relative positions eg. should not the Analysis Mercury face be on the left because when we look at it we are facing the right? Should not the Moon be down and Saturn be up? and so on.
8.3 Only when such doubts as those in 8.2 are dispelled can one proceed.

9 STRUCTURAL ANALYSIS - 3

9.1 What can we make of a 3x3 grid.

9.2 Graphology offers one answer with its analysis into:

	PAST	PRESENT	FUTURE
UPPER			
MIDDLE			
LOWER			

This could be a useful scheme.

9.3 Numerology. I have seen the numbers one to nine ranged in a 3x3 box (as in Austin Coates' book). This might suggest a meaning for the 9 positions.

9.4 Astrology. If only, as in C.F Russel's Holy Cube, we had a 4x4 division we would be laughing. However we do not.

HUMOROUS ASIDE 2: Therefore we are not laughing

9.5 However reference to NOTE 1 means that so long as we always replace the cube in its correct orientation as determined by the middle square of each sides, then that middle square can be discounted as just a "marker".

9.6 This reduces our 3x3 to a square of eight squares.

9.7 SCHEME A. Ascribe the 4 sides of the square to the four elements, and the 3 small squares on each edge to "cardinal, fixed, mutable" and you have represented the 12 signs of the zodiac. But it is not a good scheme as each corner square does double duty - so I do not recommend this scheme unless this problem can be overcome (eg by isolating meaning according to adjacent squares on other faces).

9.8 SCHEME B. An eightfold scheme. Ascribe the middle of each side to an element and the corners to their synthesis, eg:

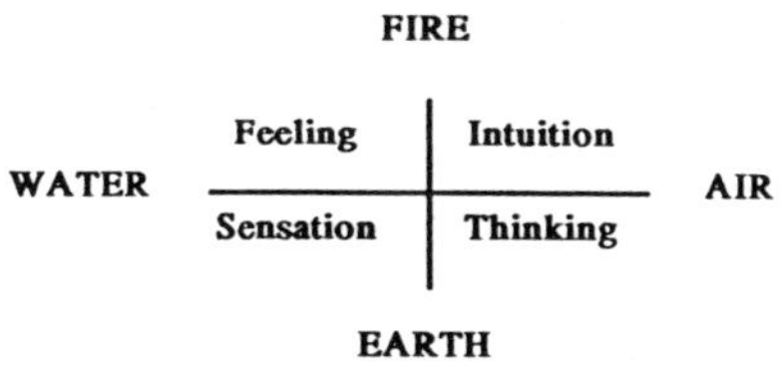

or some such scheme.

9.9 SCHEME C. Use 8 house astrology, as described in the Handbook for the Humanistic Astrologer. This would mean that a certain coloured face would represent the corresponding "planet" upon the cusp of the appropriate house, as follows:-

8	M.C	6
Asc.		Desc.
2	L.C.	4

9.10 Here is the most promising scheme. However it is again not *directly* relatable to 8 house astrology because

a) in our system any "planet" can be repeated up to 9 times.

b) only one "planet" can be on any one house.

HUMOROUS ASIDE 3: Though the Handbook for the Humanistic Astrologer is recommended for researches, do not look to it for snappy interpretations of our cube. For example a yellow square in the upper right corner would represent Mercury in the '6th'. Just grab an eyeful of what the HHA has to say about this placing:-
"The individual's mind and associative perception should be involved in the creative release of self through relationships"!
Does this mean you will meet a tall, dark stranger, I wonder?

10. USING THE CUBE

10.1 Should we always begin with the cube in its original state?

HUMOROUS ASIDE 4: Do you know how to get back to its original state? - ho, ho.

10.2 Stuart Kaplan suggests a tarot divination should always begin with a tarot pack put into its correct order. This is a "magical" viewpoint corresponding to a banishing ritual before the divination. I suggest that a more purely divinatory viewpoint would be to see all previous shufflings as part of a continuum of change.
10.3 So you may decide not to restore the cube between questions.
10.4 Formulate your question and bear in mind which type of question it is according to the distinction in para. 7.
10.5 Jumble the cube as you ponder the question.
10.6 When feeling satisfied and ready place the new jumbled cube squarely on a table before you.
NOTE: Depending upon your chosen system of interpretation (see para.9) you will have either placed it randomly or 'right way up'.
10.7 Your immediate answer now lies before you on the "Front" face. Interpret it according to your intuition bearing in mind the following factors:-
A) Certain colours in certain positions
B) A preponderance of any colour
C) The same colour in 2 or more "houses" forming a link between those houses
D) Any obvious patterns in the colours.
10.8 The answer can be enlarged upon by considering the other faces, eg. "LEFT" for past influences, "RIGHT" for future, or for logical advice, and so on. The type of question (determined in para.10.4) will decide whether all sides are to be considered. If they are then "FRONT" could mean the situation as you see it and "BACK' the situation as OTHERS see it. And so on.
10.9 Other possible interpretations could stem from viewing the six faces as opened out into a cruciform 'net' of the cube, and so on.

11. CONCLUSION

11.1 The Hungarian Magic Cube lends itself to divination as it is a

portable, clearly legible permutable set of elements with a definite structure and with suggestive links with traditional symbols.
ll.2 Up to a point interpretation of the oracle is obvious. However the interpretation of each face is radical. Several possibilities exist, but the model needs considerable intuitive exploration before it can be accepted as a new system of divination.

HUMOROUS ASIDE 5: If anyone has the time to explore this why not contact me c\o Revelations 23 Press, and we will get together to create the first standard textbook of cube divination. Remember: *I have no time!*

The eskimo shaman born aloft by an eagle - he or she had access to a world of magic that is the envy of many contemporary occultists. But remember that the primitive world was a place of uncertainty and hidden danger; insofar as the original aim of magic was to tame a hostile environment, who should be considered the better magician: the primitive shaman or the average citizen of the twentieth century? Have we really lost our magic? Or have we simply become so good at it that we suffer nostalgia for a more uncertain and uncontrollable past?

5 - MAGIC IN THE EIGHTIES - WHERE TO NOW?

First published in Arrow 13

I recall being quite pleased with this article, which was an expansion of the theme of a talk I gave in Hemel Hempstead.

FOUR ILLUSTRATIONS

Please read these four illustrations carefully, and compare your reactions to them, before reading the rest of the article.

1. The spate of public interest in UFOs, telepathy, metal-bending, dowsing and other paranormal phenomena continues, but it has not left us with a single body of evidence that is capable of standing up to rigid scientific scrutiny.

2. A friend laments the decline of a mutual acquaintance: once the finest young ritual magician around, he has now given up all such interests and seems content with respectable bourgeois pursuits like money-making and the yacht club.

3. Crossing the street from my classroom, deep in thought: suddenly woken by a screech of tyres. A car had appeared, crazily slewed up onto the pavement. (Appeared? Had it driven by, it would never have registered on my awareness; but as it was my *memory* reminded me that I had seen it coming along the street.) "Are you all right?" Nobody hurt, but one front wheel sagged out at a horrible angle. "Jeez. Lucky that didn't happen a minute earlier - we were doing 70 on the bypass" - the driver was now looking down at the wheel, while I crawled under to look.

"You won't repair that in a hurry - king pin or something has gone right through," I said, dusting down my clothes. He was looking at me rather warily. I wondered why, until his wife pointed her hand out of the window and asked "Is this Eton College?" "Yes. I teach here, that's why I'm dressed like this," I looked down at my wing collar, white bow tie and tail suit, realising how odd I looked, all the more so since the fact that these clothes were working clothes rather than special occasion wear meant that I had not thought twice about crawling under a car in morning dress. "Oh, that explains it," said the driver, looking relieved.

4. Most of the old vegetable varieties, apparently so flavoursome in the memories of sentimentalists, will soon be no more. Take peas for example: repeated tests at the Institution laboratories showed that, once they had been processed and canned, or frozen, not one of the control group was able to distinguish consistently between the different varieties. So it makes sound sense to concentrate on those vigorous varieties most profitable to the grower.

REACTIONS

If you did read these illustrations carefully as suggested, congratulations - you are a more conscientious reader than I usually am! But how did you react to them?

Statements like the first illustration irritate me; but, more importantly, they sadden me. Why? Because I know they are true. A lot of popular writing on the paranormal gives a very different picture, it suggests that science is crumbling under the onslaught of evidence. But the truth is that science is only crumbling *at the edges:* if you study the hard-core scientific reaction to the paranormal you will find little or no change. Even John Taylor has withdrawn a lot of his evidence. Does this mean that "I don't believe in" the paranormal? No: as is argued in 'Thundersqueak' and in an earlier article in this series, what I do not believe is that scientific scrutiny is the Gateway to Ultimate Truth. Instead I believe it to be a simple but extremely effective method of banishment: the state of mind we evoke when we say "let us look at these facts again very closely" is one which forms a magic circle of certainty around us, a magic circle expressly designed to exclude all mystery and surprise. Try it next time a ghost is troubling you - it works more powerfully than the pentagram ritual. So any attempt to produce laboratory evidence of the paranormal is analogous to trying to persuade a clergyman that God created evil, by evoking Beelzebub within the holy ground of his own church - the attempt is doomed because such evil is excluded from that holy ground.

The second illustration could be depressing, especially in the wake of the first one. Together they add up to a picture of the failure of the revolutionary hippy dream now that we have woken to the harsh reality of the 80s. (In fact this illustration is not needed till later in this article)

As for the third illustration: you may not know how to react to this until it is put in context, and you know how the writer intends to use it.

So what about the fourth illustration? This type of statement annoys me. Why the hell should good vegetables be slaughtered on the altar of Economics? If processing does destroy the difference, my solution is not to give up tasty vegetables but rather to avoid processing them - let's eat them fresh so we *can* enjoy the difference! Do you agree?

REVELATIONS

To return to the third illustration and its purpose: part of the reason it was included was simply to separate the first and fourth ones with a lot of words! Having confessed that, I would like to look back at the first and fourth and put them side by side in our minds to see what happens.

Does my reaction to the first illustration overwhelm my reaction to the fourth one; so that they combine to form a dismal picture of the invincible technological Juggernaut, crushing all nature and magic in its path? Or does gastronomic pleasure carry more weight than my regard for scientific truth? In the latter case I might now see the first example as exactly analogous to the fourth and come to a similar iconoclastic conclusion: "if no evidence for the paranormal is never capable of standing up to scientific scrutiny then, rather than live without evidence of the paranormal, I would choose to live without recourse to scientific scrutiny."

In purely practical terms that conclusion is not so very revolutionary: after all, how many of us really do use the scientific method in everyday life? Even in a high technology environment it is seldom used: in fact the full weight of scientific ritual working is usually only deployed in the face of danger, for example when testing safety equipment, testing a revolutionary new hypothesis or - above all - in paranormal research. So scrapping science should be easy - but it is not. For however seldom our 'rational' society actually uses the scientific method, it still treats it with slavish respect. This is even true of those of us who dislike the method and will argue against it at every opportunity. Just imagine that a surgeon has examined your child and announced that only an immediate operation would save its life, while a clairvoyant has told you not to let the operation take place: in the face of public opinion and conditioning how many of us would dare to refuse the surgeon?

Of course I would not suggest "scrapping" science, I would only suggest that we could remove the scientific method from its pedestal and put it carefully away as a useful tool in case of real need. (If the pedestal now looks a bit bare let's put 'Fun' in the place of honour.) However, the very fact that this resolution would be all in the mind means that it would not be easy. To show how deeply the old ideas are entrenched in our thought I will now explore a little further.

THE MAGICAL CHILD

Recently I read "The Magical Child" by Joseph Chilton Pearce (who wrote 'the Crack in the Cosmic Egg'), and found the book full of interesting and important ideas. (To be honest, I did wish that it had been written or presented in a style that conveyed a little more of the magic that the book certainly implied. I suspect a similar criticism could be made of my work. The themes in 'The Magical Child' could well have done with the arty-crafty, ecologically-aware, hand written, full page illustrations on re-cycled paper treatment. I am not joking.)

If we use the word 'education' in the very broadest sense, to include not only the whole upbringing and psychic environment but also the conditions of birth and even the prenatal experience; then the main message of the book could be crudely stated as follows: 'every human has a natural capacity for magic, but traditional education in our society crushes that capacity and destroys it.'

This idea is well in accord with the opinions of most occultists. For example I have heard it said that there is more magic in primitive societies than in ours because they have not cut themselves off from nature as we have. It is also often said that the best mediums or psychics are found among simpleminded or backward folk, because their very lack of intellect has saved their innate psychic abilities from being swamped by rational logic. Recently it has also been noted that the most able metal-benders were youngsters, and it has been suggested that this is so because such children have not yet had their psychic abilities educated out of them.

All these examples carry a similar message, but how does science respond to this message? Simple! of course those kids produce the most puzzling results, for we all know that mischievous youngsters are more interested in fooling adults than they are in obeying the strict disciplines of scientific method in order to discover the truth. In any case, being immature, children are more likely to be carried away by their imaginations aren't they? What about primitive societies? Well, without their having the benefit of our superior knowledge of the universe, we can hardly blame them if they too get a little carried away by their imaginations. As for those mental defectives .... say no more!

Two different views of the same facts: let us call the first view the 'Romantic' one, the second view the 'Classic' one, and put them in the boxing ring to see which wins!

CLASSIC v. ROMANTIC

There is no doubt in my mind that the first round goes to the 'Romantics'; for they win hands down on *style.* Their argument touches on my golden nostalgic memories of childhood's magic moments. It also links with our dreams of the Golden Age, the myth of the Noble Savage and so on. Beside that the 'Classic' argument seems arrogant, insensitive, tactless and boring. So on to round two.

Good grief! After that clumsy start the 'Classic' argument has scored a knockout in round two! This is so surprising that it calls for some careful explanation.

Throughout the 'Romantic' case there is a common idea of Nature being vanquished: the natural magic of childhood being crushed by convention, the natural psychic abilities of mankind having been castrated by the dogma of rationality, and so on. This idea appeals strongly to me as it has an obvious parallel with the picture of Nature's destruction by technology, put forward so vividly by the ecology movement. This idea has a strong appeal to my latent mothering instincts, but it has a weak spot in that it makes absolutely no appeal to my not-quite-so-latent religious instincts. I want to *worship* Nature, not protect her! I look back to previous centuries when Nature was spoken of as a mighty and terrible power, when men spoke of the 'majesty' of Nature and the 'forces' of Nature - protecting butterflies feels a bit tame in comparison. Returning to the Romantic argument, I find it hard to respect man's Natural Potential when I am told that it has been so thoroughly defeated by reason, by convention, by education and so on.

So how do I 'beef up' Nature to make her worshipful? I do so by expanding her beyond the small view of Nature as 'all pretty flowers and furry creatures that technology is threatening'. In the larger view man is included in Nature; earthquakes, comets, supernovas and the primal big bang are also included in Nature. On this scale there is no question of 'Man versus Nature' for man is just one of Nature's little experiments: and if Nature has chosen to mold mankind (by means of technology) into a club with which to batter the flowers and butterflies to death then it is sheer impertinence on our part to suggest that this means that Nature has somehow 'made a mistake'. Similarly it is impertinent to suggest that man's rational mind (another of Nature's creations) has somehow managed to destroy the Nature in us. A Goddess may perplex us, torment us, or destroy us, but she does not make mistakes. Least of all does a Goddess depend upon us to keep her alive. (It is my Religious Spirit speaking: Rationalism would argue against that last sentence of course!)

(In practice, despite my feeling that the Ecology Movement has helped to debase Nature in our minds, I still support it like mad - and refuse to buy goods wrapped in paper bags whenever possible. Just how I reconcile religion and daily life is material for another article - better still, another lifetime - so I must return to the point without satisfying your curiosity on that topic.)

I declare that the Romantic argument lost the second round because it made the rather silly suggestion that Nature, who created us, has made the mistake of allowing us to develop ways of life, ways of thinking, etc. which have defeated Nature herself. In comparison the Classic argument does at least have the decency to suggest that Nature's progress is right - that adults *do* know better than children, that advanced civilisations *are* an improvement on earlier ones, that clever people are *not* defective, and so on.

As referee I am far from impartial, I'm afraid. Despite my grudging respect for the Classic argument I do not like the company it keeps, for it is too often associated with the argument that Magic does not exist. So I feel that I must produce a new argument that is equal to the Classic argument in round two, yet which fits in better with what I want to believe.

THE THIRD APPROACH

A cheer, and Ramsey 'The Crusher' Dukes enters the ring!
'Why are simpletons more psychic?' shouts the crowd.
'Because they are simpletons' answers Ramsey.
A puzzled silence.
'Why are children better at bending metal?' shouts the crowd.
'Because they are worse magicians' mutters Ramsey.
Eh?
'Why was there more magic in olden times?' shouts the crowd.
'Because mankind was not yet very good at magic' sighs Ramsey.
Has he gone crazy?

What is Ramsey trying to say? If we begin with the last question which asks why there was more magic in olden times (or in primitive societies for that matter), the reply was not that primitive people are better magicians, but that they are worse. This seems a crazy statement, but let us look at it without preconceptions, and ask ourselves what was mankind's original incentive to do magic. Was it not inspired by the wish to control the environment and gain greater security? But it is surely arguable that mankind's present problems partly stem from too great a feeling of security: our environment has been tamed to the point that we feel obliged to create silly weapons and invent ideological enemies in order to put back the excitement in our lives. So a Martian observer might be forgiven for feeling that it is modern man who is the better magician, for it is a modern man who has more thoroughly tamed his reality.

If we now reconsider the first question we can imagine how the Martian observer would look upon simple-minded psychics. Instead of seeing them as people with an extra ability of their own, the Martian might see them as people who had less control of reality, as incompetent magicians whose magic circles were leaky.

If you are still not convinced, look back at the third illustration quoted at the beginning of this article. Even though I was not in that car - I was the schoolmaster - the incident scared me. Novice drivers soon learn to come to terms with certain levels of risk - if you thought every oncoming driver was likely to go mad and ram you, driving would become impossible. They learn to trust their judgement. At the time described my own judgement was not prepared for the possibility that, in these days of sophisticated engineering, stringent safety measures and yearly MOT tests, a car could fail in such a lethal fashion without any warning (had the car been going more than 15 mph it would certainly have rolled over). The sight of that torn member disturbed me so deeply that, five years later, it contributed towards a rather illogical decision to trade my car for a motorcycle. (Note also that the driver was disturbed by my clothing until an explanation had been provided.)

Our modern way of life would be unbearable if we could not depend upon metal to behave itself. Sometimes when I was driving I used to think of Uri Geller and wonder whether my fears about the front wheel linkage might not create just the right mental state to cause the metal to snap by telekinesis. It never happened, but rather than accept this as evidence against telekinesis, I took it as evidence that it was my Unconscious Will to survive. This idea is supported by the following experiment: sometimes, when feeling suicidal, I have chosen a clear stretch of road (out of consideration for other users), shut my eyes and fully opened the throttle of my 1000cc motorcycle. In a few seconds of bellowing machinery and arm-wrenching acceleration, existence begins to regain its charm: and my eyes spontaneously open to reveal that I have steered accurately while my eyes were shut (note to my disciples: this variation of Spare's Death Posture is strictly for Ipsissimi). My Unconscious Will to live has been invoked and has overcome the Conscious Will to suicide. Indeed I have a theory that it is the Unconscious Will that is the final arbiter as to who *is* going to be killed on the roads - and not the Department of Transport. Remember that in the third illustration the car did not collapse until it had slowed down: this fits my own experience that vehicles have a genius for breaking down at the most awkward or embarrassing times, yet have an equally uncanny knack for preserving life. Hence the unusually high proportion of motoring stories which end with the words: "if it had happened one minute earlier, I wouldn't be here to tell the tale". I had better leave this subject, for I would feel a right idiot if tomorrow saw my remains being hosed off the tarmac....

When the subatomic structure of matter is considered, it appears to be so insubstantial as to suggest that the real miracle is not the bending of metal by telekinesis, but rather that we are so ready to trust our lives to its not bending. Observing the extent to which human belief can shape human reality, I am tempted to suggest that the strength of metal is not so much innate, as a consequence of our Unconscious Will to preserve our own security. (Study the history of metallurgy in this light and you will find that man's inventions tend to run one step ahead of the materials needed: copper is easily mined but too soft for weapons; mix it with tin, an even softer metal, and you get bronze - which is harder!) So the child that can apparently bend metal by telekinesis is not really displaying magical powers so much as a magical failure ascribable to immature ability - it has simply failed to keep the metal rigid.

Primitive mankind cannot have felt as secure as we do in their world - where a wolf could turn into a man or a neighbour's curse could sour the milk - so the same argument would suggest that they witnessed more miracles not so much because of a superior magical ability as because they had not developed their magical powers as completely as we have. Similarly the medium who sees spirits and hears voices is not displaying a special talent lost to ordinary people, only a weaker ability to banish those spirits in order to preserve everyday reality.

What of my second illustration, quoted at the beginning of the article, of the young man who 'lost his magic'? We now have an alternative interpretation of this story. In those glamorous days when he was apparently such a great magician, he was in fact just a young seeker, in search of his true path. Now he has found that path and found, in the accumulation of money and status, a greater certainty and security than he had before. For now his magic is really working.

IS THIS DEFENSIBLE?

So that is my argument, but I bet you don't feel satisfied by it! It seems a denial of all the dreams and hopes of the occult revival; it makes magic sound so boring. 'That cannot be the truth about magic,' you say, 'because if we really were such brilliant magicians, we would surely not be feeling dissatisfied, and be searching for more of what *we* call "magic".

Really? Is this not just what one *should* expect? Is this not just the well-worn story of the success that turns sour?

Have we not all heard of the self-made millionaire who ends his life in dreams of the good old days when he shared a flat in the slums, or of the simple country girl who married an international tycoon and spent her life dreaming of the folks back home, or again of the pop star who committed suicide? Johnstone always stated that the deepest rut of all is success. Now the war is over we spend a hell of a lot of time reminiscing about it: the peculiar yearning for a return to insecurity has been aptly described in French as *nostalgie de la boue.*

When I finished my training and was going to teach at Eton my fellow student teachers tended to think I had copped out: "doesn't your conscience tell you that you should really be teaching in a deprived area?" they asked. This question made little sense to me unless the asker really believed that money solved all problems - that rich people never needed help. As it was, the difficulties I encountered at Eton were no more superficial than problems I had previously encountered in my more humble existence. In fact I sometimes felt a special calling to try to tackle the miseries that beset, for example, rich Californians because I feel these problems are not as trivial as some people claim. What, I ask, is the point of trying to raise the rest of mankind towards affluence when we have not yet tackled the problems of affluence itself?

This then I propose as the problem of our age. It is not that we have developed abilities which have cut us off from our natural magical inheritance and left us high and dry in a technological desert; instead it is that our very magic has become too good. Encapsulated in the Victorian Scientific world view we have a model of reality rather too perfect and secure for our own highly developed magical ability. We have shaped the world too successfully and mankind is now looking back wistfully to the good old days when we weren't quite so good at holding it all together and life had more surprises. Nature has not made a mistake, she has merely, as ever, striven to excellence.

THE OCCULT DREAM

Could this be the reason why the occult dream of the 60s has been so slow to realise itself? In those heady days many would have predicted a parascientific revolution before 1982 - what became of it? I referred above to the "Victorian scientific world-view": although the leading edge of scientific theory has long since moved into much more mysterious territory, I feel it is the Victorian idea which still dominates popular thought. People have heard of the uncertainties of subatomic physics, but basically assume that it is all going to be nailed down sooner or later to present once more a nice mechanical picture. Indeed, returning to the idea of Unconscious Will, it looks as if recent advances in science are a response to the Unconscious Will of that small section of the population who could not accept the narrow materialistic view, whilst the failure of those advances to shatter materialism is a consequence of the more widespread Unconscious Will to preserve our security.

If we had been right in believing that our present state of rational materialism was a mistake, an evolutionary sidetrack now needing to be retraced, then surely it would have been easier to bring about the occult revolution? If we had been right in our early assumption that we only had to become as little children in order to 'enter the Kingdom of heaven', then surely individual enthusiasm would have carried more of us across the abyss? Instead there are an awful lot of people still wondering where all the magic has gone, and too many people feeling disappointed that all these years have passed and we have still not seen the scientific establishment on its knees before Uri Geller, begging for forgiveness.

I suggest that the reason that the 'mistake' was so difficult to put right is that it never was a mistake, but rather an excess of success - and the deepest rut of all is success.

THE AQUARIAN REVOLUTION

I have heard it said that we are living through a revolution; that mankind has discovered that it has lost its balance, lost its contact with Nature, and is now turning back to the right path. I do not believe this: when an individual makes such a fundamental discovery about his own psyche it does produce a revolution, and I would expect the same in society. But I do not see signs of revolution, instead I see signs of festering: much more reminiscent of the individual whose success has turned sour than of the individual who has seen the light. The revolution has not failed - it simply has not begun. True, there have been changes in public opinion, but they are only the slow undramatic changes that accord with the slow evolution of the Unconscious Will: although many of us *want* the paranormal, we still *need* the security of materialism.

So if I can now talk about the Aquarian Revolution in the future tense, rather than in the past tense, what will it demand of us? Will it require that we turn back and abandon our left-hemisphere, rationalist stance?

To return to the analogy of the individual, the question is this: should the miserable rich man abandon his wealth to become happy?" Traditionally the answer is 'yes' - but I disagree (except in cases when the wealth is abandoned in my direction). That affirmative answer is based on two popular myths: a) 'He gave up all his money and spent the rest of his life happily helping the poor'; b) 'He gave up all his money and devoted himself to spiritual progress'.

Really these are two versions of the same story: the 'spiritual' version is based on the duality of material goods versus spirit, the 'political' version is based on the duality of wealth versus poverty. In each case the erroneous idea is to believe that misery at one end of the scale implies happiness at the other end. Anyone who tries this as a formula is liable to remain imprisoned in the duality: for example the rich man who 'drops out' in search of enlightenment, yet ends up chasing spiritual progress in just the same way as he used to chase purchasable goods.

The falsehood of these two myths depends upon a subtle shift of emphasis. Consider the man who supposedly became happy by abandoning his wealth, then helping the poor: I suggest that the truth was that the rich man, while still rich, became very interested in helping the needy; so much so that he happened to lose his money in the process simply because it no longer concerned him greatly - for he had expanded from the duality of poverty versus wealth. However, to the rest of mankind, who are still trapped in that duality, the *first* thing they notice is the lost of money and so the story goes out that the rich man found happiness by giving away his money and helping the poor, rather than the truer story that happiness was found by helping the needy - with the loss of wealth as an incidental effect. The same applies to the spiritual case: although it is easy to find quotes about rich men not getting to heaven and the need to abandon wealth and so on, I would guess that this is very much a test of the faint-hearted. The loss of wealth should be incidental; if it is done too soon and too deliberately you are liable to retain a hang-up about the act, and become the sort of spiritual disciple who thinks 'I'm bloody well going to get my Nirvana before Brother Fred, because his Daddy paid for him while I gave up my Lamborghini to follow Mahatma Kote'.

Applying this free moral lesson to the problem discussed earlier: I feel the need for a revolution, but I do not feel that it will come about by looking back along our evolutionary path. It is tempting to discourage early literacy in children (because literacy represses 'right brain' thinking) and so try to make the children more 'magical', but I do not feel this is the answer. What is needed is a new direction rather than an undoing of past mistakes.

THE NEW DIRECTION

The true revolution comes when you break out of an old duality, not when you change direction within it. What we need is a new philosophy rather than an attempt to recapture lost magic by resorting to wholefoods, real education, restoring earth-contact and so on. Such admirable pursuits are best adopted in their own right rather than for ulterior motives or for theoretical reasons. I, for example, am keen on whole foods: I choose wholemeal bread because nine times out of ten I enjoy it more than white bread; thus I am happier. If I had chosen wholemeal bread on grounds of health, I would become a victim of medical debate and those researches sponsored by the Bread Board to prove that sliced white bread is the only safe food on the market. If I had chosen wholemeal as a gesture toward 'small is beautiful' economic theory, I would remain forever trapped in economic debate. (As it is, I remain for ever trapped in my pursuit of sensual pleasure ... you cannot win!)

That is why, in *Thundersqueak,* and in this series of articles for

Arrow, I have put emphasis on new forms of belief. Those articles on Johnstone's Paradox were not so much an attempt to present a new Truth as to find a new Hope.

The first illustration at the beginning of this article suggested that none of the evidence for the paranormal could withstand scientific scrutiny. Two typical reactions to such a statement are: a) 'I always knew this occult stuff was nonsense', or b) to react angrily and take an anti-science stance. Neither reaction offers any escape from the science-versus-occultism duality. Instead I suggested a change of attitude which amounted to saying 'GREAT! At last we have a choice before us! No longer the victims of 'magical' forces, no longer (at last!) the slaves of scientific dogma: this illustration informs us that inconvenient paranormal phenomena can be safely banished by adopting a scientific attitude! The future of mankind can include a higher form of magic now that we have learnt to banish properly.' In this way the dualistic tension is released, science is removed from its pedestal and put aside as a useful tool; we are free and better armed to explore the future.

CONCLUSIONS

I have here and elsewhere in this article tended to use the word magic in two senses: in a popular sense to refer to the primitive, insecure state that is the opposite of 'science', and in a higher sense which sees science as a tool in the service of a greater magic. This is the same distinction that Crowley intended when he adopted the word 'magick' for the greater sense.

So I will summarise my theory thus: 'as long as we chase after magic, Magick cannot progress.' And I present this prediction for the coming Aquarian Revolution: 'In the sixties we became disillusioned with scientific, rational thought. In the seventies we devised an "alternative" - but it proved too weak to topple the monolith. In the eighties *we shall call rationalism/science an "alternative" and it will be its turn to fight for survival.'*

POSTSCRIPT

If a diabolist is a person who reverses the fundamental symbols of the age - saying the Lord's Prayer backward and inverting the crucifix in times past - what does that make me?

In this essay I began by proposing that we elevate 'fun' above 'scientific method'; went on to suggest that the ecology movement might be debasing Nature; dared to put forward the idea that primitive peoples and children are inferior; outraged decency by hinting that Oxfam might better devote its care to the wealthy; and finally suggested that the Aquarian revolution had never begun.

So appalled am I by this revelation of mine own wickedness, and such is the momentum of my sinfulness, that I feel impelled to commit yet one more atrocity: an act so base that the very editors of *Arrow,* nay Hugo l'Estrange himself, would shrink back in horror from its witness. For I feel bounden to fall meekly to my knees, clutching the Good Book to my breast and raising my eyes to heaven to pray for forgiveness for my evil deeds; and to surrender this most perfidious essay to the tender loving mercy of the Lamb of God by placing it naked before my readers that it may be stoned to death as is most fitting for the redemption of its fallen soul.

6 - THE TWILIGHT OF THE BLOKES - A MASCULIST REVOLUTION

First published in Chaos International 6 & 7

The original of this essay was written at the beginning of the 80s and was to be the first of a series of sketches for a "Masculist Column" which was intended to do for sexual politics what Hugo l'Estrange's "Satanist's Diary" does for the occult (bugger all?). But good taste prevailed and the series never found an outlet despite several attempts to revise it.

While preparing this collection I came across some of the Masculist Column on an old archive tape, and was able to salvage this version. I was not sure whether it really belonged in the collection, but Chaos International have since accepted it for publication as a Ramsey Dukes article - so here it is.

I recall a conversation in the early 70s with an Australian history graduate who lamented the fact that women played so small a part in history. To me that seemed to say more about the limitations of history than about the limitations of women's role in society - surely a history of food or of clothing would be dominated by women as much as a history of science or politics would be dominated by men?

To that the Australian replied that I had unconsciously revealed my contempt for women in the form of an assumption that "food and clothing" was their rightful domain. This surprised me, who had always considered food and clothing to be on a level with science, and all three to be vastly more important than politics. We are what we eat, and politics is only a vital matter at times when it addresses itself to the provision of food and clothing for the needy. Far from my demeaning women, I felt that the other had revealed an unconscious contempt of matters I considered to be "feminine" by undervaluing them relative to "masculine" matters.

As a history graduate she found it hard to accept that I did not equate formal history with ultimate truth so much as just an arbitrary way of looking at the world, devised by men in order to justify their antics. As far as I saw it, the fact that women played a lesser role in such history was not surprising -- in fact it was positively to their credit.

Conversationally we had reached an impasse. I had divided life into two categories, the "masculine" and the "feminine", and was perhaps gallantly but not deceitfully claiming that I tended to value feminine activities somewhat higher than the masculine activities which I felt were often compensatory and shallow. The history graduate valued my "masculine" activities most highly, and felt therefore that I had insulted her sex by classifying them in that way. Society as a whole seemed to over-value those activities, so Might was not on my side. The conversation ended: it had lost its potential value as a passport into her knickers... for she was a very beautiful history graduate.

The conversation left me with a sadness that went beyond the sorrow of missed romance: it revealed how mine own ideas were out of kilter with the norm. Did that mean I was deluded? or could my ideas be "better"? In either case I still had to face being the odd one out. This essay attempts to explain my view: perhaps putting it down on paper will reveal its strengths and weaknesses more clearly.

TWO'S COMPANY

I begin with a general tendency to classify everything as "yin" and "yang". In this I am fairly conventional, seeing yin as dark, earthy, watery, heavy, nourishing, peaceful... and yang as light, fiery and airy, inspiring, dynamic...

Next I assume that both those qualities are of equal absolute value, and that both need each other and can only exist because of each other. Here I am still fairly conventional, but recognise that there are people who would disagree and who believe that yin is innately inferior to yang and that life's purpose is to purge oneself of the former and aspire toward the latter.

Next I translate yin as "feminine" and yang as "masculine". This is where trouble begins, because many people then jump to the conclusion that I therefore believe women cannot be fiery, inspiring and dynamic. To explain why this is not so I need to make an arbitrary distinction of distinctions by defining "male/female" as separate from "masculine/feminine". The former is the everyday distinction between men and women, the latter is a distinction between underlying factors.

The fact that I see masculine and feminine (yang and yin) as being equal valued and utterly interdependent is reflected in the way I see them tightly interwoven in the fabric of existence. Consider an analogy with positive and negative electricity: it is almost impossible to demonstrate one or other in isolation, because every atom of matter contains both positive and negative components, but that does not mean that the positive/negative concept is not a very useful one. Pure yin or pure yang cannot be demonstrated in real life, certainly not in the form of any individual woman or man, and yet our understanding can be enriched by the careful use of these concepts.

I therefore see an individual human being as analogous to an onion with many layers within, and each layer alternates in polarity. This is again a fairly conventional view: the Jungians claim that a man has a feminine soul (anima) while a woman has a masculine spirit (animus), and so on. So a "male" is masculine on the surface, but has a feminine soul, and the feminine soul has a masculine spirit, which in turn has a feminine soul and so on ad (practical) infinitum. While a "female" is feminine physically, masculine ethericly, feminine mentally, masculine spiritually... and so on, depending how one labels the layers of the onion.

That is a tidy masculine model of how I see things, and it is easy to fault it with practical exceptions. To explain why this is so I need to exercise my more down-to-earth feminine qualities. If you actually take the trouble to peel lots of onions you discover that they are not perfect spheres of concentric shells: they are full of irregularities. Firstly they can be lopsided, thicker here and thinner there. You peel off the outer skin, which is thin and brown from exposure, and it does not always reveal a perfect white interior: sometimes there is more than one brown skin, or often the next layer is partly thin and brown and partly thick and juicy and white. In places the layer can be so thin that you see through it to the layer beneath. And sometimes as you remove a layer you find not one inner surface but two or more: the onion has a double heart, a twinned or schizophrenic onion. So also you find men whose masculine surface is flaky and peeling, women whose inner spirit is hardened and exposed, men with split personalities, people with unbalanced and exaggerated strengths... That's what makes life, and peeling onions, so interesting. As it is, so be it.

Such analysis applies not just to men and women but to all phenomena. Food, for example, was described as feminine. But, insofar as it enters into a body and gives it life, it is playing a masculine fertilising role. And, insofar as the body then breaks it down and transmutes it, the food is playing a feminine nourishing role...

Take another example: you are speaking to me at a party. Words are leaving your mouth and entering my ear, so you are masculine and I am feminine. But I am taking the sounds you make and interpreting them, so I am masculine and those sounds are feminine. The result is that ideas are being expressed by you and received by me, so you are masculine as the out-pourer and I am feminine as the receiver. But the effect is that, by listening, I am making you feel important and respected, so emotionally I am playing a masculine role by giving you confidence. Now what you say has triggered off some ideas of my own, so mentally I am feminine to your masculine fertilising influence. However, by allowing myself to be educated by you, I am contributing to improving your karma, so spiritually I am playing a masculine initiatory role...

Such analysis shows how tightly the masculine and feminine are interwoven - cut anything open and you find endless layers of each - but it also explains why I still feel able to use masculine and feminine as general terms to classify things on their surface value. It explains to what extent I see the male (men) as masculine, and the female (women) as feminine, and it also explains the limitations that I see in such grouping.

How nice if all my readers were to respond to this either by thinking "yes, he has described quite adequately the way I see things", or else "gosh, what a revelation! suddenly I understand something that has confused me for years!"

What a pity if some readers instead think "I absolutely agree - and that proves what rubbish all this women's lib feminist claptrap is!", or else "typical bloody male, to build up such a cumbersome rationalisation to defend what is basically male prejudice". The first response would merely irritate me, while the second would actually hurt me, so I had better say some more on it.

I am aware that one reason it might hurt me is because it might be true - that awareness is part of the hurt. To judge whether it is true there is little point in examining the analysis itself, instead I must ask my heart if it feels good about the analysis... and it does. Now that makes me think that my Goddess Within is not at odds with my endeavors, but that is as far as it goes: for perhaps she is a jealous Goddess with an interest in putting down merely mortal womankind? Or perhaps, like a busy housewife who, in response to a husband enthusing about the significance of United Plastics bid for Consolidated Biscuits, simply says "yes, dear" and gets on with peeling her onions, so perhaps is my Inner Goddess giving no more than tacit support to a crummy thesis.

Thoughts like these alter the balance of reasons for writing this essay: it becomes less a masculine desire to teach my enlightened viewpoint, more a request for society to play the masculine role and judge me that I may know where I stand.

THOSE WHO CAN...

So, back to the conversation at the point where the lovely Australian failed to fling her arms about me and cover me with kisses.

I did not see history, as it is generally understood, to be an absolute description of the past, instead I saw it as just one of several compensatory games devised by men to justify and occupy themselves. And, whereas I felt that most women had shown perceptivity and good taste by largely ignoring this game, there were some like this Australian history graduate who were taking it seriously and feeling genuinely hurt that they had not been written into the game.

This was were I was badly out of step. Not even those women who saw history as a game would be likely to come forward to argue such in public: the general view of society in the early 70s was that history and politics and other male institutions were "where it's at". I believe that is still the general view in the beginning of the 80s. Rather than try to defend my basic thesis in an area about which I know so little, I will choose a topic that I know more about: engineering, for example.

The latest issue of "Technology" magazine (14 March '83) has the cover story "Where are the women engineers?". The corresponding article describes the shortage of engineers and argues that girls should be actively encouraged to pursue the subject. "Conditioning, stereotyped attitudes and active discouragement from studying technical subjects all add up to the human shortfall in British engineering" runs the heading. "Active encouragement" requires positive pressure on less-than-willing girls, to counter what is seen as society's stereotype that technical subjects are "un-feminine" and so not suitable for girls. "What is needed is a glamour factor" explains the article.

Now I myself believe that technical subjects are "un-feminine" or rather that they are "masculine". In view of the previous account of how intricately and unevenly I see yin and yang interwoven in existence, the reader will deduce that I see no reason why any particular woman should not therefore become an engineer, but on the other hand I am not in the least surprised that the general inclination among girls is not to study the subject. Nor would I even justify this freedom of individual choice by saying that some women are "less feminine" and should therefore be free to study engineering, for I see no reason why a woman need not be immensely feminine in all obvious respects yet still have the particular masculine mental streak that suits engineering - just as an otherwise immensely male man might still fail to be a good engineer.

In fact I am suspicious of the motives of those who deny what seems such obvious truth! Turning to page 22 in the same magazine we see a much less prominent article "Engineers are let down by their education" with the header "Survey also reveals engineers feel neglected by employers". The article describes how engineers are frustrated and under-performing because industry treats them as "back room boys" expected to solve problems while the management, marketing and accounting whiz kids take all the important decisions and get paid vastly more.

Now this does ring true of my experience in the engineering-based industries; and I strongly suspect that the feeling extends to scientists as well as engineers. Although scientists can partly compensate by associating with the glamour of those "scientific breakthroughs" that capture the public imagination, the vast majority of them experience life as "back room boffins" at the mercy of a better paid and more responsible administration.

The cover article states that girls have a "false and unattractive" view of engineering, it talks of their "in-built prejudice" against it, and their "stereotyped attitudes". The suggestion is that teenage girls are fluffy little things blown hither and thither on the winds of sexist fashion, and that a new wind of engineering glamourisation is needed to puff them in the right direction. However, the survey in the second article would suggest a second possibility: that engineering's un-glamourous image is based on reality, and that girls are making a wise choice in resisting technical subjects.

As the overall tone of the article is "engineering needs our women", rather than "women would benefit from engineering", it begins to sound like a repeat of what happened to the secretariat. A secretary used to be an extremely responsible position in the longhand days, and it remained a jealous male preserve until the advent of typewriters. As the job began to deteriorate into an endless round of mindless typing, women were encouraged to fill the role. The secretariat has now become a female preserve - and a humble one at that. So it looks as if the urge to recruit women engineers is basically another example of the male tendency to recruit women to take over any work once it loses its ''yang'' excitement and turns to ''yin'' drudgery. The fact that the article was penned by a woman does not deny this impression: as my opening example suggested, the ebb and flow of yin and yang works at many deep levels and it is a very yang simplification to reduce it to a surface ''battle of the sexes''.

Indeed, what the engineers' sense of inferiority boils down to is the simple universal rule: ''Those who can, do. Those who can't, organise those who can.''

To be more precise, but to extend beyond the industrial environment in the above paragraphs, the rule is this: ''those who can, do. Those who can't, teach. And those who can't teach, administer.'' This rule is often interpreted as a cynical joke - which can therefore be repeated but never taken seriously. I suggest that it reflects a natural order of things. Take a primal human out of the jungle and it is a pretty useless object - it doesn't have a woolly fleece, it doesn't make honey, it isn't all that strong or swift - all that Jehovah could do with such a creature in the Garden of Eden was to give it dominion over other creatures. Mankind's very lack of evolutionary specialisation has lead to our taking a dominant role.

Returning to present society: anyone who has had to endure too many lectures by ''leading experts'' will realise that a good teacher needs to be someone who can identify with the audience's difficulties: although a teacher should have a good grasp of it, the message will get across better if the teacher has also had to struggle with the subject. Again, in industry and public service I have heard it said that ''old so-and-so is too useful in the research department, we can't afford to let him waste his time on administration''. But these examples are weak rationalisations of what seems to be a fundamental and universal fact of existence - that those who have a vital ability will tend to get on with it, while those who lack such ability will tend to teach or organise others. The fundamental nature of this rule is shown by the way that it extends beyond the strict use of the words "teacher" and "organiser" into a general statement about human (and, for all I know, divine) behaviour.

When science and engineering are not on pioneering ground, they can be very un-glamourous. The respective remedies suggested in the two articles are: 1) to recruit women to take over the drudgery and relieve the men for fun jobs, and 2) to transform engineers into decision makers. I suspect that both solutions are doomed to fail in the long run because they both go against nature. There will always be exceptions to the rule "those who can, do", and there will always be women with the right gifts who feel secure enough in their own femininity to become engineers, but it would be unwise to shape policies around exceptions rather than around general principles.

I don't believe for a minute that the women who wrote the cover article was consciously engaged in a plot to exploit members of her own sex. Instead I believe that she had been brought up to think that masculine activities were better than feminine ones, so a shortage of women engineers was interpreted to mean that women were being held back from the best jobs. Whereas the other article revealed the fact that engineering is now a second-class activity, and that women can consider themselves well out of it. Just as they can consider themselves lucky not to have become a major part of man's history.

THOSE WHO CAN'T...

The trouble with the above argument is that the people most likely to accept it are the people who like the status quo and want to keep it as it is. Those most likely to reject it are those eager for change, like my Australian revolutionary. Because I prefer revolutionaries to those who like the status quo, I need to hastily move on to how I see evolutionary change in the role of the sexes.

Why are women (subject to all the individual exceptions) generally found in a subservient role? As in the case of engineers, it is surely a consequence of the general law already stated: "those who can, do". That leaves the men free to take the lead.

Remember that we are still a youngish species, with plenty more evolving to do. Until very recently the prime function of humankind has been to survive and multiply. I admit that male humans have slightly greater strength and aggression, and that this has helped slightly towards survival, but its significance pales to nothing beside the female ability to bear children. A tribe of women co-operating together would have enough strength, intelligence and skill to survive as well as most mixed tribes - provided they were not limited by beliefs about their own inferiority. Only a handful of males would be needed to provide semen for such a tribe of amazons, all further males would be surplus.

But nature has provided this surplus of males: half of mankind are virtually useless in terms of propagation. Knowing deep down that they "can't", men have devised an endless array of substitutes: art, philosophy, religion, fighting... plus of course teaching and administration (not to mention the institution of monogamy which provides every male with the chance of employment - a little kingdom of his own). Without any really important responsibilities to hold them back, the male sex has put so much into these substitutes that they now totally overshadow the original purpose of life. Like the engineers who can no longer appreciate the value in their "back room" work once they have seen the Marketing Director drive to work in a Porsche, many women have lost touch with their real importance in the light of all the glamourous phantasies men have devised. Men may rule the world, but it is women who have made it.

Women made the world? Reverence for such excellent masculine phantasies as history and science makes it hard for some people to accept that we live in a world created by women. But just look at the facts.

The world we live in is the world we experience, and the way we experience the world is programmed within the first four years of life. By the time we have learned to speak we have laid down the entire structure of reality, a reality that is merely fleshed out in later life. This basic structure is laid down in the years we spend with mother. It is a structure she gives us but, because it is laid down at a pre-verbal level, it is not necessarily the structure she would consciously wish to give us. She may have read a book on child care, full of advice on how to teach a baby, or she may be a convinced christian, but none of these conscious attitudes will provide more than a surface gloss to the deep unconscious attitudes and assumptions about the world which the child picks up from her behaviour, her moods and her gestures in these formative years.

Woman made this world, and woman made it in her own image.

The world shows every sign you would expect of an entity made by women but administered by men. If men had made this world, it would be orderly. Instead we find that just about every institution devised by men - religion, philosophy, law, politics, technology - is an attempt to impose some order on a profoundly chaotic world. The very fact that there are two sexes has a suspiciously feminine ring to it: men prefer unity and would have stuck to one sex and got it right (they would probably have had us laying eggs in warm sand and leaving them to hatch in the way turtles do). Quantum mechanics is just the latest in a long history of Nature's affronts to men's attempts to explain her away. Indeed everywhere you penetrate beneath the crust of male compensatory institutions and touch the matter of reality itself, you find the confusing fingerprints of woman.

Those who can, do. Women make this world, and find themselves enslaved by their own essential role. They are back room girls.

Those who can't, administer. Men rule this world because, poor things, they have nothing better to do. The advantage of being useless is that you are unhampered by responsibility, so you are able to put a lot into whatever compensatory activities you devise. The company director who does not have any manufacturing or design skills is free to handle the company as an abstract financial entity, so he does it rather well and leaves the more useful members of the company fuming at his glittering success. And if a man does not have any organisational skills he will still seek something to compensate for his inability to create this world: he will try to excel in art, writing, ideas...

You see, if you can't make the world, you can at least make something you call "history". Another way of creating a role for yourself is to attempt to impose some order on the chaos of existence by explaining it scientifically, or in religious terms. And if you do have a creative streak and are unable to create THE world, you can at least create A world as an artist, writer or film maker. Hero, wise man, artist, poet... men act out a myriad roles and try to forget that the clearest expression of these archetypes lies not in their lives, nor even in any male mind, but rather in the female subconsciousness. Mother has even created the stereotypes for their rebellion.

No wonder the role of mother and housewife sounds un-glamourous beside the dazzling array of masculine alternatives devised by men. No wonder my Australian friend felt hard done by.

But all I seem to have done so far is to justify the status quo. I have yet to explain why I think it is evolving.

THE GREAT MALE ROBBERY

As was suggested three paragraphs back, male compensatory roles do a good job in bolstering male esteem - so much so that women themselves envy them. They also help us to forget our basic inability. Yet they remain just a compensation for the real thing. The more you excel as scientist, mystic, artist or whatever, the more you are liable to be haunted by the realisation that you have become an example to others without having successfully quenched the basic internal hunger which drove you to excel in the first place. Sooner or later every man seems to glimpse that it is all just play. What is really wanted is the ability to make this world, to create reality.

Just as women have been relentlessly and unconsciously superimposing stereotypes onto existence - even when they consciously despise those stereotypes - so also have men been relentlessly and unconsciously undermining their own decorative status by trying to get their hands onto the creative act.

Consider the feeding bottle. It means a baby can be fed without a breast, and so it means a man can feed a baby. The way is paved for significant male intervention in those formative years. Consciously men resist this, for they have been brought up by Mother to consider baby suckling to be woman's work, yet the institutionalised male mentality has done much to force artificial baby milk onto the world. The way for change is being paved; and note how the male unconscious drive reveals itself most clearly in its institutions, whereas the female unconscious mind is expressed more clearly in moods and actions - which is the way the female structure of reality has been programmed into us in our mothers' arms.

Consider also how the male has become involved in delivery. Despite conscious revulsion by individual males for the blood and agony of the birth process, the institutionalised male has almost outlawed the home delivery. Without looking at statistics I would bet that most babies in Britain were delivered by male doctors while the mother lay in a semi-drugged state.

Consider the statistics which have been quoted as to how the modern baby spends more time in front of television (which is, we are also told, a male institution) than in its mother's arms. The baby is increasingly being "programmed" through male eyes.

Even when the modern mother does interact, to what extent is she influenced by the fashionable writings on child care? In my (fairly recent) parental days that meant books by male experts.

The more that an "expertise" in baby care is evolved, the more justified a woman feels in putting her child in the hands of experts at an earlier age. In the past that could only mean a wet nurse, now it is more likely to be a kindergarten run by a local authority according to the latest pedagogical practices.

Surprisingly, even the idea of the "nuclear family" will serve to break the seal between mother and child. The family unit (as opposed to "family" as clan or dynasty) is a modern idea hardly significant before the late 19th century and it is probably therefore a patriarchal invention, and the idea that "a child needs a family" is beginning to take the place of the earlier idea that "a child needs a mother". This paves the way for greater participation by fathers and other children in the baby's upbringing, and the original idea that a nuclear family demanded a full-time mother begins to take second place as the concept of "family" grows stronger in its own right.

There is still a long way to go toward the test-tube baby which makes no demands at all on the woman, and yet men are beginning to sense that their old dreams of homunculi and the creation of life are growing closer, while women are beginning to get a corresponding sense of what it means to be redundant. And this is where the evolution feeds itself: because of that unconscious sense of growing redundancy, that loss of certainty about woman's vital creative role, an increasing proportion of women will feel the need for substitute glories. Rather than resist the male usurping of the creative role, they begin to welcome the chance it gives them to indulge more freely in those exciting substitutes they have so long envied. They would actually prefer to go back to work than to stay at home and bring up baby!

In a world made by men, it would be women who would feel driven to justify themselves by teaching, by administrating, by being artists, mystics and seers. Men would now be too busy to do anything but envy their exciting games.

MALE PRESERVE US

The change I see beginning to take place is that babyhood is becoming less and less a female preserve as men get their hands onto those formative years. Already men are beginning to play a small part in creating the world and this involvement will accelerate as the possibility of relieving busy women of pregnancy and creating test-tube babies grows closer. I also see little female resistance to this evolution, because the other side of the coin means a lightening of female responsibility for existence, coupled with a drive to compensate for very deep feelings of redundancy, and this will mean an exciting new era for women. Any resistance to this change is more likely to come from men who find they are increasingly involved in the back-room labour of world-creation. Like those dejected engineers, they will tend to overlook the fact they are now more valuable than women, and will merely envy the glamourous games women will begin to play.

The immediate temptation is to see this change as a gradual but basically straightforward reversal of roles: a future where women dominate existing public positions, the Law, the Arts, Education, the Media... a world like ours except that women make the history while men are heavily involved in mundane technological husbandry. A world with plenty of exceptions of both sexes, of course, but no more so than there were in the man-administered world. But we should consider a little more carefully before accepting such a simple idea. Would you really expect women to start going to war just as men used to?

Remember, we are now considering a man-made world: not just a reversal of roles in our present world. So what would be the characteristics of a man made world as distinct from the traditional woman-made world?

Adolph Hitler's vision of the Third Reich is probably a good starting point, as is Huxley's Brave New World. The first example seems frightfully unattractive, because it is tainted by memories of the horrors perpetrated in an attempt to create the ideal envisioned by Hitler. Why were the means so appalling in view of what must at least be acknowledged as a well-meaning end intention?

The answer of course is that the basic ideal of the Third Reich was not in itself that bad, it is just that a chaotic woman-made world refused to accept such regimentation and the frustration of trying to impose order reduced the Reich to brutality. This is an archetypal pattern: the more a creed or philosophy has "order" as its aim, the more thuggery and chaos it will invoke. The Thatcher government came in on the "law and order" promise, and has invoked more violence than ever. Scientology is a movement that initially promised to create order in our minds (the aim being to become "clear" of all tangles in one's psyche) and yet something very similar to a brutal fascist state was created in the movement. And the most far-out movements of the sixties, like the Manson Family and the Process, had roots in the scientology philosophy.

The general rule seems to be this: if you try to force order on the world - whether by a Law and Order legislation, by military pressure, by psychological coercion or whatever - the world will react in such a way as to brutalise you. The reason for this is because it is still largely a world made by woman in her own image, and it resists regimentation.

So what would happen if the world was man-made? In that case it would not be fundamentally a chaotic world. In place of Heisenberg's Uncertainty Principle there could be no more than a Principle of Slight Residual Doubt - if that. The laws of physics would be *known* in a man made world. It would be a tidy, neat and predictable world with well ordered weather: no droughts, tempests or famines, except when the occasional commemorative tempest is organised in a small enclosure as a sort of public spectacle.

A man made world would be so very different. It is extremely unlikely that there will be two sexes in the future. Two is a number that is extremely irritating to men, and this fact is used by women for manipulative purposes, as in the old trick of offering two ghastly alternatives ("do we go to your parents this Christmas, so I can spend the rest of the year moaning that we never go to my parents, or do we go to yours, so I can spend the rest of the year asking why my parents always have the burden of entertaining us?"). Ideally in a male world there would be just one sex, but possibly this will be compromised by having a whole range of sexes - ultra-butch, limp-wristed fop, bearded lady, crumpet etc etc - each with its own union, regular newsletter and membership privileges. Any number except two, please, in view of the male saying "two's company and three, thank heavens, is none''. A man-made world would be a fair world, a rational world with an emphasis on clear choice in place of all the fatalistic nonsense of Mother Nature and the Norns.

Servicing such a world will be like playing a vast game of multi-dimensional chess, and it will require all the resources of male thinking. That is why men will soon be too essential to be wasted on history, politics, art and all such fluffy pursuits. In our present chaotic women-made world most things get blamed on Fate, but in a man-made world there will be only cause and effect. This will demand a huge bureaucratic structure to maintain existence, and the role of husbanding such a reality will demand all the ''masculine'' skills like accounting, engineering, programming and so on. Whereas women used to be trapped in the vital role of ''housewife'', men will find now themselves trapped in the equally vital world of ''worldhusband''.

So what will women do? What sort of roles will they create for themselves? There will, of course, be a temptation to take on the old male roles: to become lawyers, policemen, scientists etc. But insofar as those roles were an attempt to impose order onto chaos, those roles will rapidly become redundant as the man-made world comes into being. A fair, liberal world full of ''sensible'' people would not need policing in the same way that the present world needs it. The need will not be to impose order onto chaos, instead it will become necessary to bring some rhythm and flow to a world that is increasingly in danger of crystallising and stagnating.

This is a role that women would identify with. As an example of a man-made microcosm (within our present woman-made world) consider the bachelor flat, or the gentleman's club. Although the former might not look tidy, it will have a basic underlying order to it - there is probably a precise relationship between the placing of the piles of washing up in the sink and the number of days it has been there. Few things give women so much satisfaction as to be able to sweep into such a world and revolutionise it with new furnishings, and a frenzy of re-arrangement. This, then, will be the underlying theme of the part women will play in a man-made world. Instead of trying to impose order onto chaos, they will be trying to invoke chaos into the order.

Taking the police as example: instead of a group of men

patrolling the streets to discourage unruly elements, there will be women going around trying to stir up community activities in a world where most people increasingly want to sit quietly at home and watch television. Even if called "the police", they will be more a sort of state Women's Institute, busy organising fetes and fund-raising activities to jolly us up. The legal profession would give way to a sort of counselling service. Politics would be not so much a question of diplomatic peace-keeping as a sort of moral strip-tease to stir up a bit of passion in a complacent world *(cf Mary Whitehouse and Margaret Thatcher when she gets on her "traditional values" hobbyhorse - Editor).* The arts will be less deeply affected, because the impulse will remain the same: it will still be an attempt by those excluded from the primal act of creation to find other ways to exercise the creative impulse. And a religion dominated by female bishops would focus less on attempts to bring order into creation, and more on bringing a sense of wonderment, joy and mystery into a very explicable universe.

OVER THE TOP, LADIES!

So that is the revolution that I see. It begins with a gradual male usurping of the baby-minding role.

This in turn leads to women beginning to feel the sort of profound sense of uselessness that has always haunted men, and so they are increasingly driven to justify themselves in the world by other means. This drive gives them energy.

This in turn increases the pressure for men to take over the process of birth and, as the new generations grow up, the world is increasingly populated with people whose elemental world view was programmed by men instead of by women.

As a man-made world would be structured on rational choice and "fairness" rather than blind Fate, women will find it easier to take the chances that have so long been denied them; meanwhile men will be increasingly tied down in the tedious task of maintaining and servicing a world where nothing can be blamed on "Lady Luck" any more.

As women step into the key roles in society, they find that the world is now longer what it was, and those key roles are subtly shifting: instead of an unruly world demanding a rod of iron, they are increasingly taking over a heavily structured world that demands inspiration and excitement. Just as "little women" used to struggle to keep the home fires burning while men fought wars to conquer an unruly planet, so will "little men" be struggling to preserve their crusty institutions while women rush about invoking "change for change's sake" *(cf the impact of Thatcher on the legal profession etc - Editor).*

A REVOLUTION WITH BALLS... OR ONE THAT IS BALLS?

Now that is how I see it, but of course that is just a neat male model of what must really be a frightfully confused situation beginning, as it does, in a chaotic female world.

Firstly there will be a residual tendency for women to want to do things just as the men used to do them, having been brought up to believe that was "right". Like the engineering woman and my history graduate, they will want male roles in their traditional form.

Then there will be the tendency for men to feel threatened by this usurping of what they consider to be their roles, with a resulting resistance or backlash to be expected in the form of outbreaks of neo-butch heroism or tyranny. This backlash will weaken, of course, as male children are increasingly taken out of the hands of mothers who instinctively program these heavily polarised sexual roles.

Then there will be the confusion of the sexes already described: the women who are naturally competent in masculine activities, and the men with such a strong "mothering" streak that they bring up baby with all the assumptions that a women would have given it.

Then there will the residual exceptions: women so broody by nature that they will refuse to give up their traditional role, and men with so little inner creative spark that they will rather rule someone else's world than create their own.

In other words it will be just as easy in future to find exceptions to prove that men really rule the world, as it is has been possible in the past for some people to find exceptions to prove that, behind it all, women really rule the world.

Although the writer of this essay can find plenty of signs that this gradual Masculist Revolution is well under way, and that its roots go back to the Age of Reason when women began seriously to follow male advice on child rearing rather than placing full trust in "women's mysteries", there are just as many signs that the whole idea is a load of nonsense.

So, even if true, it will be such a confused and long drawn out process that no-one will notice it happening: each generation will accept the world they are born into and will assume that to be the natural and immutable order of things.

Therefore there is little point in this essay. Its only value is in its attempt to sort out mine own bizarre assumptions.

What do you think?

My Goddess Within just says "yes, dear"... and I see tears sparkling among the many little circles of sliced onion...

In re-presenting this old plate from The Astrologer Of The Nineteenth Century am I giving it life? or simply calling up the dead? If Jesus or a creative artist does it, we say the former. If a magician or commercial artist does it we say the latter. So what does the following essay do for Johnstone's paradox?

7 - JOHNSTONE'S PARADOX REVISITED

First published in Arrow 15

This seemed to be the essay where I finally got it right: my first three attempts at expounding Johnstone's Paradox seemed to have failed, or fallen on stony ground, but this one created some response. First it was was printed with ''disputatious footnotes'' by Mormegil Draconis. Then there was an article by Starwing to which I responded (see next chapter). Both of my letters of reply were published in Arrow 16. After that I felt Arrow must have had its fill of Johnstone's Paradox, and I resolved to put it all down in a book (Words Made Flesh, which came out in 1988). I think it was the interest generated by the illustrative story in this article which gave me the idea of including the story about the Minister for Technology and the Pope in Words Made Flesh.

Knock knock ... "Hello, you must be Johnstone's Paradox ..." "Who the hell are you and what d'you want? ... *"How are you keeping, Johnstone's Paradox? Putting on weight? Hair going grey? Teeth falling out? ..."*

The other day an occultist friend of long standing spoke to me on the subject of Johnstone's Paradox (see articles in Arrows 8, 9 and 10) as follows:

"It's all terribly neat and clever, but do you *really believe in it?"*

Isn't it wonderful what close friendship can engender? Like the story (apocryphal, presumably, for I am about to invent it) of the two Great Ipsissimi who used to meet regularly in a quiet corner of the Saville Club to discuss Great Cosmic Truths, the Work of the Brotherhood and the Worlds Beyond the Abyss. During a lull in one such conversation Ipsissimus A gazed at his coffee spoon for a silent half-minute then suddenly spoke. "There is something I have been longing to ask you for many years, Ipsissmus B. tell me, do you think you would ever be able to bend a spoon like this by telekinesis under laboratory conditions?"

So it is that a friend of long standing, and of long understanding, a friend who has read and absorbed SSOTBME and 'Thundersqueak', can still ask me if I "really believe in" Johnstone's Paradox!

My reply, which I am about to summarise, revealed that I had lost none of my old skill at evading such questions.

WHO IS THE GREAT BELIEVER?

The question of what I myself believe is not very important. The world of the future has always been shaped by those who believe the hardest, so the important question of the future age is 'what class of people are the strongest believers?

The bad news is this: occultists are definitely not the strongest believers at present. There is still amongst occultists too much looking towards the borderline of science for theoretical and evidential support; in other words they are still asking permission of science to believe in magic. (The slightly nervous questions about the distinction between Black and White Magic that persist in public meetings show that there are many who are also still asking permission of religion to believe in magic.) And in my last essay, on Magic in the Eighties, I gave the example of the ardent occultist who finds a beloved one is on the threshold of death, and who has to choose between orthodox medical advice to operate and a psychic's advice not to do so. How many would uphold their occult beliefs in such circumstances?

I would propose two candidates for the Hardest Believer Cup. One is the American Bible Belt Creationist. I do not have any direct experience of this group, so will pass it by for the present. The other candidate is the 'hard-headed' rationalist, the 'goats' of the Society for Psychical Research. You need only read the anti-paranormal writings of such people in, say, the correspondence columns of *New Scientist* to realise that here are believers of the first magnitude; here is a rock solid defensive position that would need rather more than Flower Power to break its walls.

The mortar that holds these walls intact is exceptionally strong because it consists of a very basic, elementary philosophic assumption, a principle of universal economy called Occam's Razor. This principle, crudely expressed, says that the fewer things you believe exist, the better.

Two examples show how this works in practice. First consider creation: if science can definitely prove that the known laws of physics were capable of bringing about the Big Bang, creating stars, planets, forming our earth and developing a life upon that earth which would eventually evolve into mankind, then there is no need to believe in a Creator who formed me in his own image as described in Genesis. We already believe in the laws of physics so, provided they can do the job, we do not need God as well. Secondly consider spoon bending. If we restrict ourself to reliable filmed evidence of spoon bending, and a professional conjuror points out that there were moments when the spoon was out of sight, and that (by taking advantage of such moments) he is able to duplicate the feat by trickery; then there is no need to believe in telekinesis. For we already believe in human deception, we even believe that this sometimes takes place unconsciously, and we already believe in the unreliability of hearsay; therefore we need not also believe in telekinesis.

This principle is then the binding strength of the rationalist position. It owes its strength to the fact that it is such a simple, fundamental principle that it tends to be taken for granted rather than consciously used. It is almost more of an instinct than a philosophical principle. Notice, however, that its greatest strength is as a defense of the status quo. However militant and attacking the skeptic sometimes seems, his position's real strength is defensive. For it begins with (for example) the laws of physics as the accepted belief, and then decides that we do not need God. Anyone who had never heard of physics, but who did believe wholeheartedly in a God who was a bit of a handyman, would be quite able to use the same principle to dismiss the laws of physics as unnecessary. So why does this not happen more often? The answer is that the rationalist view has dominated Western thought for about 400 years and is now so entrenched in our culture and language that even the child of the most zonked out hippy family probably assumes that, for example, sunrise is inevitable rather than being a daily gift from a thoughtful and very reliable deity.

This is why the present day occultist cannot use the same principle to such advantage. Although I have demonstrated in these essays, and in SSOTBME and *Thundersqueak,* how magical theory can provide alternative explanations to scientific theory, that are just as neat and sometimes even more economical; the arguments lose their strength because we all *already believe in* scientific explanations. We may resist this belief, but in vain, for it is, so to speak, already in our blood.

Consider the example from SSOTBME of the magician who suffers from traffic lights always being red when he is in a mad rush, and who decides to remedy the situation by meditating himself into calmness in order to reduce the number of red traffic lights to normal. The scientist laughs at his 'remedy' as a piece of psychological deception and 'proves' this is so by counting the number of red traffic lights next time he himself is in a mad rush. He finds merely an average number and so deduces that the apparent surfeit of reds was in fact a delusion, and the magician's 'magic' has done nothing. However the magician in turn can now laugh at the scientist, pointing out that the scientist had merely performed the self-same magical act: by deciding to objectively count traffic lights when in a mad rush, the scientist had calmed his consciousness and therefore reduced the number of red traffic lights to normal just as the magician had done.

Some people who read such examples of mine find them 'all very clever', but a bit out of touch with reality. I suggest that this is because, although they can recognise how well balanced my argument was, they *know* deep down that traffic lights are worked by automatic electrical systems that would not adjust themselves to one individual motorist's thoughts when there are thousands of others on the road all in different degrees of haste.

HOW DO THEY DO IT?

Granted that the strength of the rationalist position is mainly defensive, how then has it gained so much territory from magic and religion? The answer I have previously suggested is that occultists, for example, tend to waste so much energy trying to attack the well-defended rationalist position rather than getting on with strengthening their own territory; and that from time to time they fall back exhausted and let rationalism march forward.

Once upon a time physics had shown itself to be awfully good at explaining simple laboratory processes in mechanistic terms, but was still a bit flummoxed by magnetism - because this force was able to act at a distance. So occultists got terrifically excited about magnetism and created a whole magical theory on etheric forces, animal magnetism and so on, in an attempt to storm the citadel and grab a bit of that delicious scientific respectability. But they eventually fell back in disarray and the laws of physics extended to cover magnetism.

Then there was the feeling that science could not answer all questions because it could never explain Life itself. A theory was created of a Vital Force invading the dead world of matter, and again it tried to become scientifically respectable.

At each stage in the spread of the rationalist domain there are some of us who recognise the obvious fact that science does not yet know (all) the answers and who decide to set up camp on such unmapped territory. If we then turn to face science and attempt to attack from that viewpoint we exhaust ourselves in attacking a well defended position, and are eventually over run. If only our education would allow us instead to ignore science and get on with improving our own camp, then something very different might happen. We might create a new universe, invisible to science and so in no danger of being overrun.

Instead of this the retreat is continued. Science buttoned up Life, and so next the human mind was taken as the 'unmapped' territory. Then computers entered our lives and so magic retreated into the non-automatic process of the human mind. Now intelligent systems are being created, and we shift camp to the creative/mystical processes of the human mind. From a rationalist viewpoint the worlds of magic and religion are being driven back into an ever shrinking territory, and there is no obvious reason why this retreat should not continue towards vanishing point.

SUPPORTING VOICE

My exposition of Johnstone's Paradox lost some of its impact through being based upon predictions as to what computers might be capable of in the future, rather than what you can now buy over the counter. So the more I can support these predictions the better will I strengthen my case. Here then are three recent predictions from 'more respectable' sources which are relevant to my thesis.

The first is that the US government is poised to decide whether to make biological computers a national research priority. What is suggested is a form of organic computer rather closer to living matter in construction and supposedly "a billion times denser and faster" than the boring old silicon chips. This news item, quoted from "Technology" magazine, considerably narrows the gap between present-day computers and the working of the human brain.

The second comes from a television documentary on computer graphics in the aid of cartoon animation. It was shown how a computer with relevant data on human anatomy, together with an initial and final picture of, say, a man raising his hat, was able to 'instantly' create all the in between pictures needed to make a smooth animated sequence. As an extension of this useful, but limited, ability we were told of a full length cartoon film now being created, about life on a robot mining settlement on the asteroids. What was being done was to map all the features of this imaginary world into the computer's memory then to program the computer to output a visual display of any required sequence of movements within that world. Say it was necessary for the film to move the camera down the long high street towards an advancing band of menacing invaders; then, all the relevant details having been entered, the computer would produce a perfect t.v. sequence of this scene on its screen: a visual film of a totally imaginary world.

The third prediction comes from an article, in New Scientist I believe, attacking the need for manned journeys into further space. It predicted that we would be able to fit sensors onto our unmanned probes that matched our own human senses of sight, sound, touch and so on, and that the information they collected could be either recorded and brought back, or else transmitted back to earth and replayed directly into an 'armchair astronaut's' brain. He would then experience the trip just as if he had been present on it - but without the danger or the added freightage. It was also suggested that the same technique could be used recreationally: a delicate, bedridden geriatric who regrets never having gone hang-gliding in his youth could pay the current world champion to hang-glide off the top of Mt. Blanc with a similar sensory recorded on his back. It could then be replayed into the geriatric's brain and he would be right out there, the wind cutting his cheeks and ruffling his hair, the clouds swirling past, the butterflies in his stomach and the sensation of swooping downwards ... (*These are examples of what we now call''Virtual Reality'', Editor.*)

Now put these three predictions together. You have a computer creating an imaginary world, like the second one, but it is a bio-computer and so the world it creates is as finely detailed, as imaginatively rich and as beautiful as any created by the human brain. Now instead of inputting recorded information from the 'real world' into that geriatric's brain, you input information from our imaginative bio-computer. And he will find himself living a dream, in an 'imaginary' world that is utterly real to his senses.

This combined model takes us a long way towards my assumptions in the Johnstone's Paradox articles. Let me now make my own prediction. Rather than go into tedious detail for the sake of realism, I will present it in dramatic form and assume that Arrow readers are capable of abstracting the essential points of this prediction.

PREDICTION:
THE AQUARIAN REVOLUTION

It was the year BLEEP. Occultism and Religion were almost extinct. Sales of Aquarian Arrow had dropped, from eight figures, to five figures, to thousands and now the magazine offices were up for sale. Natives of tropical countries, who used to burn offerings and pray to their gods to keep storms and earthquakes at bay, now rang up the local meteoronomists and seismonomists departments and asked them to create clement weather and to stabilise the earth's crust. The early public outcry against the unimaginative and inhuman face of computers was finally quelled when critics universally acknowledged that MUZAK IV's New World Symphony made the entire output of Beethoven look like a rather tepid cup of overweak tea in a plastic beaker from a British Rail platform vending machine. The electrostatic inkjet paintings of Sylvie IX07 made Rubens look 'decidedly naive', and, since the arrival of G-KLOWN's comedy talkshow, no-one was any longer interested in repeats of such predictable and humourless programs as Monty Python or the Goon Show.

The few remaining dissident voices were being silenced. The Archbishop of Neasden, cornered by the Minister for Technology in a Soho night club, said that he was fully aware of the triumphs of science and cybernetics and yet despite that knowledge he awoke each day with a strong conviction that 'there still remains some central mystery as yet untouched by science'. 'Don't worry about it' replied the minister for technology, 'we know all about that feeling. It is caused by an imbalance in the nodular cortex resulting in an overproduction of hyperbleemoid hormone. Just take these tablets, here, and the condition will be cured overnight'. 'Ah yes' retorted the Archbishop, 'but the point is that I have no wish to cure the so-called condition'. 'I appreciate that' replied the minister, 'this second condition is also well understood. The two drops of antibolshene-3 that I secretly introduced into your last drink will have eliminated your problem by tomorrow lunchtime.'

And so it came to pass that only one non-rationalist remained, only one person who still daily praised his Creator at sunrise and invoked the Great Ones at sunset. He was mocked by a world that could not understand his faith. Why invent a divine creator when new universes were being daily created by science to entertain the masses on sensorama sets? What achievement of man was there that had not been excelled a billion times over by the digital logic of GENIAK V? But still the mystic resisted. 'You have conquered and reproduced the whole world' said he 'but you have yet to conquer my soul'. The minister for technology was just dying to dose the mystic with antibolshene-3, but GENIAK V took him gently aside and reminded him of a certain passage in a book called '1984'. Here was the last mystic in the history of mankind: for him no ordinary defeat would suffice.

So, a few months later the minister visited the mystic and invited him to spend a sabbatical fortnight at public expense in a newly created sensorama universe. 'No fucking fear, you can stuff your bloody dreamworlds' said the mystic. Whereupon the minister sighed and prepared to depart with the words 'well, you have shown me one thing. For all your defiant believing, you have not got enough courage in your convictions to test them against our "bloody dreamworlds". Unable to resist such a taunt the mystic agreed to the minister's suggestion.

The next day he was 'reborn' into a lovely land, inhabited by a people of great warmth and humour. To his joy he found that the sense of wonderment and reverence for nature was still thriving in this world. And there he met Krystal of the Seven Moons, princess of the tribe. And they fell utterly and hopelessly in love.

Now any of you who have ever been carried away by a great film, and fallen temporarily in love with the shortlived and merely two dimensional hero, or heroine, will perhaps understand what happened to that mystic in his blissful fortnight spent breathing the same air, treading the same earth, sharing the same laughter with that most perfect embodiment of everything he adored.

And having yourself walked alone from the cinema into the wet streets and the queues for buses, will realise how the mystic felt on being recalled from his sabbatical.

'I wanna go back'

'But come now,' the minister smirked 'surely you cannot want to trade the real world, the world given to you by your beloved Creator, for one of our "bloody daydreams"?'

'Yes, I do'

'But all that you have experienced is merely permutations of digital information input by our scientists, even Krystal is just a program'

Jerked into tears by the mention of that name the mystic sobbed 'Whatever she is I want nothing but to share that reality with her.' His was the age-old dilemma of the princess who falls in love with the gipsy, or the lord who falls in love with the exiled courtesan - only a little more poignant.

'Well, if you insist,' sighed the minister for technology. 'But you will have to sign a refutation of all your beliefs before you go - we cannot have anyone saying that we had coerced you, can we? It just happens that I have a copy here...'

And thus it came to pass that the last mystic was eliminated from the universe. The worlds of Magic and Religion had been squeezed into a smaller and smaller space by the creations of Art and Science. [I have especially worded that sentence for those who have read SSOTBME and who will see its additional significance]. Now that shrunken world has imploded and the result was...

A BIG BANG !

For what had been proved was that there is absolutely nothing in our universe that cannot be re-created in a sub-universe by an ordering of information in this universe. But by Occam's Razor this means the number of universes must be limitless.

Now, wait a minute, surely Occam's Razor does not encourage us to believe in lots of universes when only one is needed?

The point is that we have already created a second universe in this story. Occam's Razor tells us that time is limitless, unless we have already located its limits (for why otherwise believe in those limits?). So once we have shown that we can create a universe we either accept that this has happened indefinitely already, or else we have to believe in some special 'principle of exclusiveness' that makes us the one and only first-time universe creators. Although Occam's Razor would prefer fewer to more universes, it is actually powerless to restrict the number. This is because a 'principle of exclusiveness' would add a whole new dimension to the space of possibilities, whereas a multiplicity of universes merely extends a dimension that has already been shown to exist. (Just as the skeptic finds it easier to believe a whole armoury of deceit on Uri Geller's behalf - including a radio receiver in his tooth - than to believe in a tiny bit of psychic power).

As a result, we have shown it can be done, we must now either prove that it has not already been done, or else believe that it has been done 'often'. In other words it is now very unlikely that our own universe was not itself created by beings of another universe which lies 'outside our time and space' quite literally. And the burden is now on the rationalist to prove otherwise.

Note that future generations in Krystal's world will have a myth on the lines of 'angels of God the Creator who found the daughters of men were fair and sought to lie with them. For this they were banished from the Kingdom of Heaven'. That will be their version of the Minister's little ruse. But does not such a myth already exist in our own universe?

I did mention that the other group of hard believers were the creationists, didn't I? They too would shape the future if we let them.

JOHNSTONE'S PARADOX

This then is my scenario for the Aquarian Revolution: an explosive rebirth of mystical wonderment following the compression of the worlds of magic and religion into the black hole of Johnstone's Paradox.

My previous articles have explained why this event would utterly turn the tables on rationalism; but, to refresh your memory (and I fear that such refreshment is called for) here are some examples.

Let us say you are creating a universe, a sophisticated version of that cartoonist's world described earlier, and you need to create a field of grass. Now there are fifty-three million grass plants of different sorts in that field - are you going to laboriously program each one in turn? Not when you remember that each and every grass plant is a vastly complex organism involving highly involved chemical processes etc etc. Any programmer would advise you to work more along the following lines.

First you create an undifferentiated GRASS program, containing all the characteristics common to all species of grass. Then you create a second set of programs, one to each type of grass. For example the COUCH program will call up the GRASS program but input into it various parametric values specific to couch grass, a creeping rootstock, a certain shape of leaf and so on. But you still have not created a single green plant, not until you go to the next stage and create programs for each individual plant. For instance COUCH 1397 calls up a file of information about the soil conditions at location 1397, it then inputs this into the COUCH program, together with information from a file on meteorological conditions, and the nature of neighbouring plants, and the resulting output is a complete description of the grass plant that would grow in that position. Thus you have created a field of grass by the most economical means: to have programmed those plants independently would be a ludicrously uneconomical deployment of information.

Suddenly a being from your created universe walks into your created field. It treads on the grass plant at location 1397 and breaks it. It bends over and calls upon the 'soul' of the plant to forgive this act. It stands upright and with eyes half closed addresses itself to the 'couch angel' and promises co-operation. Then throws up its hands in ecstasy and hails the presence of the Great Archangel of Grass. And you, the creator of this world, are falling about with laughter.

For you know that the whole grass thing is just a nifty bit of programming; so all this rubbish about 'souls', 'angels' and 'Archangels' splits your sides.

But think again. What does the being mean by the 'soul' if not the reality that lies behind the manifestation? It has merely given a name to the program COUCH 1397, and called it the 'soul of this plant'. What does the being mean by the 'angel of couch' if not an archetypal immaterial couch plant, and would not the form of that 'angel', were it perceptible, be the form of a perfect couch plant undifferentiated and unstunted by any contact with actual material conditions? In other words, it is the program COUCH.

Similarly what is the Great Archangel of Grass if not the program GRASS?

This suggests that, once we have accepted that our own reality is probably a programmed creation, then the principle of economy no longer says 'manifestation can be explained without the assumption of angels, gods and souls, therefore we shall not believe in them'; instead it says 'a world created without angels, gods and souls would be so absurdly uneconomical that the onus is no longer on the believer to prove that they exist, but on the unbeliever to prove that they do not'.

I am told that a biologist called Rupert Sheldrake has written a book in which he postulates an 'M-field' that psychically links all beings of the same species: so that if a germ in Australia for example learns something the information may be instantly transmitted to a similar germ in England. Apparently the horrified reaction of the editor of Nature was that the book ought to be burned for suggesting such rubbish. But once the universe has been seen as a programmed creation then the onus would be on the editor of Nature to prove that no such link exists. Because a world where nearly identical entities were in no way linked by a common program would be such an absurdly uneconomical world that Occam's Razor would barely allow it. For it is not the 'M-field' which would be the redundant hypothesis, some such connection is inevitable in the nature of such a universe; no, the redundant hypothesis would be the mysterious 'principle of isolation' apparently demanded by the editor of Nature. Why on earth should such a principle exist? In this model the mystic's feeling of 'oneness' is the obvious truth while our everyday sense of isolation is the greater puzzle.

Similar arguments to show the inevitability of astrology, all systems of divination, reincarnation and so on have already been given in my earlier articles. The point is that once our universe is seen in this new light, then the whole of magical theory is no longer an outlaw fighting for breathing space outside the reach of Occam's Razor. Instead it becomes the fundamentally acceptable 'truth' and the mighty old rationalist viewpoint is suddenly the outlaw.

This then is the nature of that magical Big Bang.

LETS FACE IT CHAPS

O.K., lets cut out the airy-fairy speculation and be utterly pragmatic.

Those of you who try to believe in higher worlds, occult powers and the like ... doesn't it just break your heart that no-one has taken up the Great Randi's challenge? a cheque for several thousand pounds for anyone who can convincingly demonstrate paranormal powers? Doesn't it just break your heart every time human achievements are belittled by the achievements of machines?

Then become a champion of Johnstone's Paradox! The only occult theory that makes you feel better every time that the scientific establishment deals magic a crushing blow! The only occult theory that is specifically designed to survive the collapse of all occult theory! Vote for Johnstone's Paradox!!

What theory could be more in keeping with the spirit of the Aquarian Age? For the Big Problem of Aquarius (symbolised by the Leo-Aquarius opposition) is the problem of the individual versus the collective. How can the individual find its place in the collective without loss of individuality? But, as I explained in an earlier article, Johnstone's Paradox will transform this dilemma. Being part of one vast programmed creation ensures a definite position for the individual within the collective - there can be no 'outsiders'. But on the other hand it dramatically increases each individual's significance. As I explained in that article, there is no longer any theoretical reason why a lonely meditator on a mountaintop cannot find out as much about the universe as can a multi-million pound government research program. Being parts of a Whole gives us all equal access to the Whole, however humble we may be.

So do I 'really believe in' Johnstone's Paradox? Well, I try. And it pays.

BEWARE OF TEMPTATION

Talking of the Age of Aquarius - well I was, even if you were not - I must give a warning. Beware of thinking as follows:-

Ramsey Dukes is a nobody of no great magical attainment, so I'm blowed if I am going to believe his crummy theories.

This is the same error as the one which states that, because Aleister Crowley was obviously no saint, therefore Crowleyanity is a wicked thing to believe in.

Aquarius is the sign of the Collective, so the old principles of the cult of personality may no longer be relevant. To take a rather flattering example for comparison: as far as I know Einstein, for all his clever theories, could not split an atom to save his life. All the old "if - you're - so - clever - then - why - aint - you - rich ?" tests of respectability may no longer apply. It may now be necessary to judge a theory in its own right rather than in the light of its expounder's saintly bearing.

There are at present thousands of prophets, all tuned into different wavelengths and all receiving different versions of the truth, and I am one of those prophets. If Johnstone's Paradox prevails it is unlikely to be because I become the world champion sick-healer or spoon bender. Instead it will be because more and more people just happen to tune into the same wavelength. Einstein has profoundly influenced our view of the world, but he never made a single atom bomb.

Well goodbye, Johnstone's Paradox. Thanks for the chat and it's good to see you looking so well.

-Ramsey dukes

John Hancock, born 1896 at the Cape, spent his boyhood in Canada, his teens in the English Midlands, and the last year or two of his life in London. He drowned himself in Regent's Canal at the age of 22, leaving a considerable body of poems, essays, allegorical stories and drawings - including this one published in The Golden Hind Vol I No 2. The title reads:

"GOD OF ISRAEL, THE FIRST GOD STATE CREATING FROM HIS BODY ADAM & EVE, THRUSTING THEM AWAY FROM HIM THAT HE MAY CONTINUE HIS INWARD TURNING SEARCH FOR HIS GOD, WHO IN THE FORM OF A WINGED SOUL IS FLYING INTO THE BEYOND"

8 - THE STARWING DIALOGUE

First published in Arrow 16

The last Johnstone's Paradox article (Johnstone's Paradox Revisited) actually prompted a live response. Firstly it was printed in Arrow15 with editorial footnotes added by Mormegil Draconis, and secondly there was an article by Starwing in the same edition raising interesting questions about the story of Krystal and her relationship with the Last Mystic. Arrow 16 contained two substantial letters from Ramsey Dukes, the first replying to Mormegil's footnotes, the second replying to Starwing's article. Both were printed as dialogue with further responses from their respective addressees.

The Starwing letter is long enough to count as an article in its own right, so it is included here for the sake of completeness. But the limitation of space means that the Mormegil dialogue and Starwing's own words have not been included. Curious readers will have to get hold of the relevant back issues of Arrow (numbers 15 and 16).

From Ramsey Dukes

Dear Starwing,

Thank you for your interesting and flattering comment on my Johnstone's Paradox article. What had I in mind for the relationship between the Last Mystic, his image in the 'dream world', and Krystal?

In the early sixties I heard a talk by Gregory in which he suggested that future computers, of some form or another, would be able to reproduce the human mind. By this he meant that it would for example be possible to hold conversation in depth with such a computer and have no way of telling that you were not speaking to a human being. The next step, he suggested, would be to model an already existing human being. But how could such a model imitate my every utterance, gesture and reflex perfectly, unless it also possessed an identical consciousness of self? In other words my mind would now be existing within the computer.

So what I was imagining in my story was a computer of such ability, but larger so that it could contain the consciousness of a whole world of beings, together with a model of the world they inhabited. This was Krystal's world and, to her, it would seem very bit as real as our world does to us. But to the Last Mystic it was just invisible information flow in the interior of a computer, until he 'materialised' into that world. This was done in two stages: brain scanners read the information from his brain into computer memory and his mind and body were then modelled by the computer, which then devised a suitable entry into Krystal's world (e.g. descent from a flying saucer) that would not do violence to the laws of that world (i.e. would match the existing programs). Secondly the Mystic's body was isolated and replaced with sensory input from the model within Krystal's world. This ensured that the memory of the experience would be recorded in the physical brain; if this were not done the two (initially identical) minds would diverge into two different minds as physical body and computer model lived out their different experiences. Then the Mystic descended into Krystal's world and lived there until the flying saucer came back for him a fortnight later (in Krystal's time). He then returned to his physical body with all the usual amount of memory recall of his fortnight's holiday, plus a few bruises and other "psychosomatic stigmata" resulting from the struggle to get him to re-enter the flying saucer.

But what about Krystal? Once the computer had had the input from the Mystic, it did a "computer-dating" job and sought an "ideal" partner from Krystal's world. With a whole planet of beings to choose from it did a superb job. (Had none been sufficiently close to the ideal it would have been able to arrange one anyway by selective breeding, for the timescale within Krystal's world was not necessarily the same as ours: so a few generations might pass in an hour or two.) Krystal was a "best fit", rather than a perfect Anima, because it was desired that the Mystic should fall in love with someone within the existing dreamworld. To have created a whole new world to contain a perfect Anima for the Mystic would have been a bit expensive, and to have created and entered an Anima into the dreamworld would have meant that the love affair would have been between two 'angels' rather than an 'angel' and a 'human': this would have made it less poignant.

Having explained a little more clearly what was in my mind when I wrote the article, I have "answered" your comment insofar as it would have been conversationally impolite to have remained silent. But also recognise that you have raised other more basic questions and that the answers to these may never be known by me: in fact, thanks to your reply, studying the implications of Johnstone's Paradox is no longer the lonely preserve of one man. So may I take this opportunity of writing in more general terms, to encourage others to research along these lines?

First a point of clarification that is very obvious, but can be overlooked by those who miss the early argument: Johnstone's Paradox says absolutely nothing about the way in which our world was created, why it was created, its relationship with the other reality, whether we were created consciously or by accident, or whatever. All it says is that, if the reductionist "nothing but" theory of the universe eventually triumphs, then, instead of destroying Mystery, it will suggest an even greater Mystery. This is because it would then seem that our universe is not "real" in any absolute sense, but is an image created by the ordering of information in another universe which lies outside our space and time.

That is where Johnstone's Paradox begins and ends. The fun starts when we (arbitrarily) accept the conclusion and see what possibilities it opens up. This interesting line of meditation I recommend to Arrow readers. Basically you can set off in three directions, but each casts light on the other. You can re-study scripture, history and myth in the light of the assumption that this world is as described above: this ''academic'' approach throws light on a lot of puzzles. Or you imagine how future people in our world might use their ability to create new worlds: the ''science-fiction'' approach is a great creative exercise, and throws up delightful parallels. Thirdly you can explore the possibilities in a purely abstract, philosophical manner. Here are some examples of questions posed by the last approach. Was there ever a first universe from which all the others have descended? If there was, was it a complex universe like ours, or was it a universe of unimaginable simplicity (like the original binary universe of Spencer Brown's ''Law of Forms'') from which increasingly complex universes have evolved? If there was not a first universe, but an infinite chain, is that chain evolving with time, or is it an unimaginable circle (the serpent eating its tail) so that the last universe ever creates the first universe - outside time. Another question concerns the existence or not of free will in this programmed universe; and was our universe created deliberately by conscious being(s), or did it evolve automatically from the previous universe? Then what is the relationship between the universes? Does a higher universe react with, manipulate, or enjoy feedback from a universe it has created?

This philosophical enquiry throws up a multitude of possibilities, and very few obvious restrictions. One way of sorting this multitude is to move to the academic approach, and study existing evidence to see how it supports these possibilities.

Begin by the simple assumption that our apparent reality is in fact an illusion created by information programmed in a different universe outside our space and time, but let us make no assumptions about the possible beings that created it. Even this very simple assumption throws a lot of light on certain debates. For a start it gives a new understanding of the traditional view that the world of matter is all illusion. As I explained in the second

Johnstone's Paradox article (Arrow 9) this simplest assumption justifies synchronicity and all systems of divination, it also supports reincarnation, telepathy, telekinesis; and in the forth article (Arrow 15) I explained how it supported the concept of angels, archangels and gods that permeate our reality. Again, in the third article (Arrow 10) I showed how the bizarre and apparently paradoxical findings of particle physicists seem much less bizarre when you ask yourself what sort of discoveries might be expected to be made by beings in a programmed reality when they tried to analyse the basic elements of their reality.

Now extend your exploration by considering the possibility that beings from a higher reality might be able to interact with our reality. The curious behaviours of flying saucers - the associated folklore of "men in black", telepathic communications and paranormal phenomena - all make more sense if we see them as invasions from a higher universe, rather than from a far distant star. Similarly all the "chariots of the gods" theories of Von Daniken can be retold, with certain paradoxes resolved, if we assume that those early settlers came from the higher universe, rather than from our outer space. If you accept the evidence of advanced scientific thinking that is reflected in ancient structures like Stonehenge, and wonder why such mastery did not lead to an early technological revolution, one answer is that these structures were designed by shipwrecked astronauts from a higher civilisation who were doing their best to exercise their higher intellect in the crude world in which they were trapped. But this answer poses other problems: why no remains of their vehicle? Why no return visits before the TV cameras or reliable witnesses? So let us replace these stories of spacemen with the story of a higher universe that became overcrowded (or otherwise uninhabitable) and whose inhabitants chose to abandon their old bodies and continue their consciousness in new bodies within newly created universes. Then may of the old problems are resolved, for these travellers came from "outside of space and time".

Next one can reconsider mystical writings in the light in the possibility that their writers may have gained some awareness of the true nature of our programmed universe, but bearing in mind that they lived in the days before computer science had given them a language with which to describe this awareness. In the second article (Arrow 9) I considered the creation theories of Rudolf Steiner, and of the Kabalists, in the light of this idea. I also explained such themes as the birth of Christ, divine inspiration and the meaning of one's True Will.

Finally let us turn to the ''science-fiction'' approach. Think what we might do if we were able to create subuniverses, and see what the results would be. In the forth article (Arrow 15) I told the story of the Last Mystic, and pointed out how his descent into the subuniverse left it with a myth about angels and the daughters of men which sounds strikingly like the one that already exists in our world. So let me leave you with my latest science fiction future, and I will emblish it with italicised comments to explain how our decisions when creating a subuniverse cast light on certain metaphysical problems which haunt the denizens of that subuniverse.

The Brave New World had arrived. World government had abolished war, technology had abolished famine, controlled the elements and eliminated crime - well almost. You see, there was a snag. The population density was such that nearly all available space was required for food production, and life extension demanded a very low birth-rate, because of the relatavistic limits to space colonisation. As a result there was a very stable society that was a haven to those too stupid to ask for more than food and entertainment; it was also a haven to those evolved sages who needed peace to explore their inner selves and to aspire to mystical bliss. But it was hell to a middle class who were clever enough to want challenge, but not clever enough to create their own challenges. This middle class was a potentially dangerous, disruptive element that could all to easily resort to crime unless there was some way of elevating them by education.

How used an army to train its men? By setting up assault courses to force them to tackle hardship. But no assault course could ever match a solo battle against the elements, so soldiers used to be abandoned in the wilderness armed with only a knife and a groundsheet. Surviving a week in these circumstances taught things that no ordinary assault course could teach. All the same, no soldier was ever fully fledged unless he had some experience of active wartime service.

So how could this dangerous middle class be educated? Challenge them with elaborate assault courses, devise competitive team games and you educate them up to a point. But what can take the place of the Outward Bound school? There was not much real challenge in climbing Ben Nevis in January anymore, because firstly the weather men no longer allowed dangerous weather there; and secondly the whole mountain was covered with pheronome sensors which could detect a frightened human and automatically launch a robot rescue helicopter within seconds. (This system was necessary to protect the hordes of trippers). So how can we present a real challenge in such an ordered world?

The answer is to devise the ultimate 'total commitment' assault course: an "Outward Bound" universe!

The universe that is created is a harsh one, with "nature red in tooth and claw" *(cf. the problem of Evil).* Evolution was directed towards the creation of a suitable android vehicle - the " homo sapiens" *(cf. "man created in God's image". Also Steiner's suggestion that archetypal Man pre-existed in a higher world, so that physical animals can equally be viewed as incomplete or overspecialised fragments of the human (mystical view), or as evolutionary forerunners of the physical human (scientific view).).*

Once a human species was evolved, how was it to be used? One possibility would be to allow your trainees to control a human body like a puppet. This might be educational, but it would be no more than a glorified "board game". It would be better for the trainee's consciousness to enter into the human body, to feel its physical pain and pleasure. This would be to use the world like an assault course; a much better educational experience, but still limited because the mind would know it was just an assault course and would be likely to commit suicide or otherwise withdraw when the struggle got too bad. But there is a third possibility: to leave the mind of the human as it is, but to mount it as a rider mounts a horse. This is the greatest challenge because it leaves you with a vehicle *(the human being)* that is utterly committed to its world, it puts the rider in a very close relationship with the human *(yet without damaging the human's essentially "earth-bound" nature because a) the rider is utterly dependent upon the vehicle and at its mercy, but b) the rider has the possibility of 'taming' his vehicle and gaining a measure of control over it.)*

So this is how the middle classes were educated in a specially constructed "school of life". Depending upon the individual's record to date he would be allocated a certain level of handicap in his next round or "incarnation" *(Karma from previous incarnations).* El Vismit, for example, had a series of rather tough incarnations (as a slave in Athens, as a poor Celt under Saxon invasion, as an Elizabethan street minstrel) and had learnt a lot about resisting hardship, but had developed rather antisocial habits. For this and other reasons he was told he must now endure an incarnation into a family of idle-rich socialites. So El Vismit studies the form for a while, weighing up the various vacancies, seeing which which fit him best, which offer the greatest challenges or chances for Karmic improvement, and eventually puts in the highest bid for a particular foetus. So Elvis Smith was born into Hollywood's jet-setting Smith family. Elvis was, for reasons of genetics and early background, a rather tough and antisocial character. This is why El Vismit chose him: a compatible nature would be more open to communication. But this caused a lot of problems in his socialite childhood milieu and Elvis became rather violent. El Vismit found himself on a bucking bronco during Elvis' teens. But after dropping out of high-school, and a disreputable year of petty crime in slum areas, Elvis found himself drawn towards social work. This was El Vismit's first big success: one reason why he had bid so high for this incarnation was that he saw all along that once he had got Elvis' body out of his family circle and into the slums, then he had a chance to communicate with it *(or giving it a glimpse of its True Will).* A long hard struggle developed between Elvis, his chosen work, and his family background. One thing that encouraged him (though he never told anyone else) was an old gypsy clairvoyant who told him he had been an Elizabethan street minstrel, a poor Celt, and a Roman slave in former lives. Before he died, Elvis at last managed to reconcile his family to his social work, and some of the family fortune was diverted into charitable trusts. This restored El Vismit's Karmic balance considerably, but El Vismit was still sorry that another incarnation had passed without the body having any real Knowledge and Conversation of its Holy Guardian Angel: Elvis had begun to sense El Vismit, but had never actually realised him.

It took two more incarnations before El Vismit managed to awaken his steed, and another five before he managed an almost totally conscious incarnation and lead a human being into Buddhahood. Then and only then was El Vismit wise enough to be released as a free citizen of his own world.

Note that El Vismit had to pay for his incarnation: the currency was Karma, and even the meanest incarnation costs a lot. El Vismit's less advanced brethren might have to opt for an animal incarnation for more elementary practice. Very incomplete souls can often enter Elvis' world in a purely abstract capacity as spirits or demons. But the most sought after prize is a human incarnation *(cf. Jung's VII Sermones which suggest that the Gods are many, but men are few, and that numberless Gods await the human state)* and these discarnate spirits will try to grab the reins if they can *(cf. possession and obsession).* The horse and rider analogy is perhaps a good one, but I do not think that El Vismit has the power to dismount before death: he is utterly committed and is at the mercy of his own failure. Elvis is well able to resist El Vismit and follow his "lower" nature alone, but he will do so under difficulty, feeling the jerk of the reins and the pain of the spurs but without understanding their message. If these obstacles, and the subtle sense of aimlessness or dissatisfaction goad him into some measure of co-operation with his 'higher self' *(cf. individuation)* then a greater sense of purpose arises. But a life is not necessarily any easier, because El Vismit has his own Karmic debts to pay: you do not break in a horse in order to leave it grazing, but in order to fulfil some task. The more this co-operation is developed the more Elvis becomes one with El Vismit *(cf. the development of a soul that can reincarnate as described by Gurdjieff: it is not the lower Elvis that will reincarnate, only that part of him which manages to identify with El Vismit).* A very advanced being could hit jackpot and reincarnate consciously *(cf. some Buddhist ideas).* Note also that there is co-operation rather than rivalry between those, like El Vismit, in human incarnation: the more enlightened humans there are the better chance each rider has of taming his steed in this or future incarnations.

So that is one theory thrown up by the Science-fiction approach. I mentioned early on that the three different approaches are complimentary and can cast light on each other: my italicised comments give give some idea of how this approach could provide insights to fuel the academic approach. Two examples will illustrate how the academic approach can cast light on this model: the myth of Atlantis and the concept of the Devil.

The myth of Atlantis suggests that, in prehistory, there was a precociously advanced civilisation but that it turned bad and was virtually wiped out. This would suggest that the first attempts by our creators to "enter" our universe were misjudged. Once the world had evolved a suitable human vehicle for their purposes, they begun by doing the obvious thing: instead of forming an unconscious link with the human mind as suggested, they entered into a conscious rapport and lived directly in the human mind. This produced a much more dramatic raising of consciousness, and this terrific evolutionary boost led to a technically and socially precocious civilisation in a primitive world. Unfortunately they did not make sufficient allowance for the strength of the minds they had entered, the strong feelings that had evolved in their created universe, and this "lower nature" in some cases overwhelmed the higher mind that had entered it. This corruption spread and caused the collapse of Atlantis. But the lesson was learnt: from then on the higher mind stood behind the scenes in the unconscious and directed the evolution of the lower mind in this slower, but in the long term safer way as suggested in the El Vismet story.

Now about the Devil...... My basic assumption all along is that the programmed ordering of information leads to the creation of some form of consciousness. So the world that was created is itself a conscious entity; this consciousness is the 'supreme god' of that world. Now the creators of this world initially had their own plans for its use, but unfortunately their creation proved rather wilful, it would not co-operate and began to cause trouble in their world. As 'punishment' for this pride, or for their own protection, they cut off its inputs into their world. In other words Lucifer was cast out of heaven. In his turn Lucifer has fought back, instilled an element of his own willfullness into the most highly evolved species in the world. As a direct result of this he managed to repulse one invasion of 'his' territory when he corrupted the Atlanteans, now his creators have been forced into more subtle methods to win back their territory: they are trying to lure mankind into enlightenment. The creators have invested to much into their creation, and love it too much, just to "pull out the plug". By a cleverly low-profile guerrilla attack they managed to slip Jesus into the works despite a wholesale massacre of babies: but they only succeeded because everyone was expecting the invasion to take the form of a conquering king at that time. Now, as Mary Stewart Relfe assures us, the antichrist is once more in full control and his message is as follows:

"You, mankind are being used. This 'higher nature' that tries to 'elevate' mankind is no more working for mankind than the 'higher nature' in the flour mill which sets out to refine the flour into white flour. I, on the other hand, am one of you; I'm not an outsider, but part of the same creation. So shake off these so called 'divine influences' and follow me. I will show you that your true self lies within this world, not in some higher world. And don't worry, nobody is going to pull out the plug".

In reply our creators say "Lucifer can only look inwards, he does not know the full details of the Divine Plan we have for you. Trust us, after all even he trusts us not to pull out the plug".

The philosophical approach makes its own contribution here, by asking "was this world really created for the purpose of educating the likes of El Vismit, or was it created for some other purpose which was thwarted by Lucifer's 'fall'? If so is El Vismit's education a by-product of a genuine battle to conquer territory created by Lucifer since his fall?"

Picking with Discrimination's Medicated Chopsticks through my verbal diarrhoea, you discover that I have invented a model of our reality that offers interesting insights into the nature of creation, of free will, of True Will, of Karma, of Evil, of spiritual attainment and of diarrhoea. But I myself have so exhausted myself in the process that I have quite lost track of what I was writing about. And its bed time.

So best wishes from

Ramsey Dukes

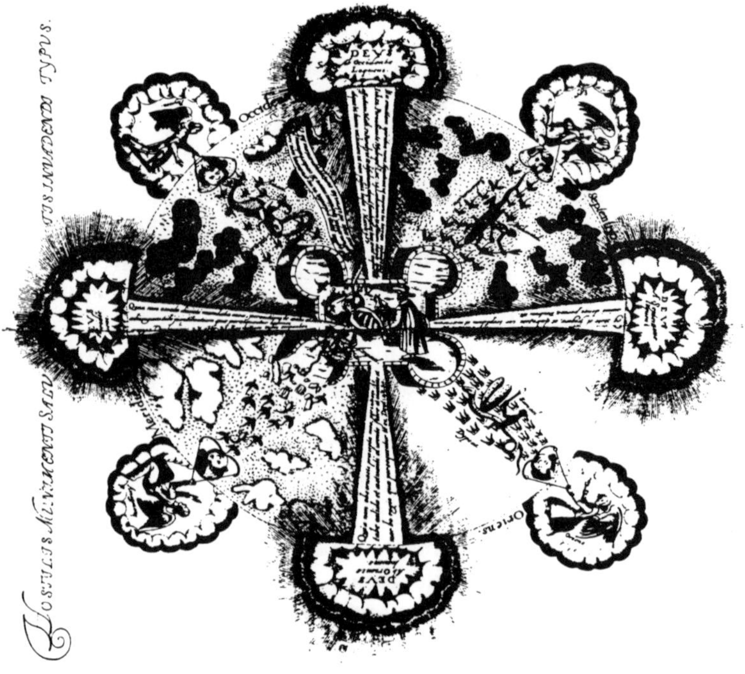

The problem with any fourfold scheme is that it tends to be resolved by our minds into pairs of opposites and this leads to conflict or rejection. Perhaps the answer is to use the scheme rather than just think about it? An orienteer makes good use of the compass without getting into tangles about the North/South divide or East/West disputes. Though some people despise neat, oversimple models or principle, the SSOTBME model in this chapter has been a useful compass to me because I never spent much time worrying whether, for example, economics was an art or a science. Yet I do recognise this problem with fourfold schemes, and in a forthcoming book will try to present my solution.

9 - CHAPTER NINE OF SSOTBME REVISITED

First published in Arrow 17

The success of Johnstone's Paradox Revisited must have gone to my head, as I decided to look back at some other ideas. In this case I chose my ropey predictions in Chapter Nine of SSOTBME to see if a bit of fudging could improve on them. I still quite like the article that resulted, though it reads like hard work.

The media's perception of the hippy phenomenon of the 60s seems quite bizarre to me, and quite out of step with observation and individual opinion. This is is typified by a cranky statement I heard on television this week: "the 60s didn't change anything - things are worse now"! (I hope the "nuclear button" never gets into the hands of people who believe that things are unchanged when you make them worse.)

I see profound changes spreading like ripples from the 60s. Mrs Thatcher could never have become Prime Minister in the satirical atmosphere of the late fifties and early sixties - her chauvinism and moral crusading would have been laughed out of court. Hippy ideology has taught us that it is ok to have principles and that you can turn back the clock at the same time as you turn it forward. The world is full of signs that people have learnt these lessons - even if many of them have responded by with principles which oppose those of the hippies, and a desire to turn the clock back to the wrong moments.

To the media there would be only one proof of success for the 60s: if we had become locked in time with no further change of fashion, or philosophy, and if psychedelic music had dominated the charts for evermore. It is the old dream of imposing the stamp of your will irrevocably on existence, and the media still live in that dream. I hear tv barons describe their hobby as "the most powerful medium in the history of civilisation", but when you ask why they show so much rubbish on television they are quick to point out that they are at the mercy of the "ratings" and the advertisers. So much for power: all I see is a deluded system tossed about like froth on the surface of deep tides totally beyond its grasp.

This old dream - of the powerful manipulator who moulds history to his will - cannot survive in face of what we know about the unpredictability of turbulent systems. We cannot now believe in the old duality of those who are working for good and those who are working for evil, because to make any change is to invoke uncertainty. The new duality is between those who wish to keep things as they are, and those who wish change. Mrs Thatcher was an unwitting avatar of chaos.

I see many changes since the 60s: the fact that they are not precisely, or even approximately, the changes that the hippies wanted to see does not deny their existence. It is often pointed out that the world is now more materialistic, rather than less so . But I do not yet see a whole-hearted embracing of the material world, all I see is a hysterical outward expression of shallow greed - the sort of reaction one would expect from a person of troubled conscience. Somewhere I wrote that the aggressive revolutionary mood of the mid-70s did not feel like genuine revolution to me, it felt more like something that a schoolmaster would recognise: society was behaving like a class of lively kids who were trying to provoke teacher into disciplining them. In the same way I could not respect the 80s materialistic attitudes: they were too much on the surface and too hysterical: they looked more like the behaviour of adolescents who had been brought up to believe in spiritual values and who were rebelling against them in order to provoke God into manifestation. They had more of the quality of hysterical behaviour before the bomb drops, than any genuine reappraisal of the values of material existence.

The gurus of the 60s have given us their messages and they have sunk home. ''Home'' is, however, far from the surface that denies it.

During 1982 I realised that the focus of my interests had shifted from occultism to the performing arts: nothing very sudden or extreme, indeed I would have overlooked the slight change of balance were it not for a growing impression that the public in general were losing their fascination with the occult. Several occultist friends were feeling disillusioned, bookshop keepers reported a drop in sale of occult books, and such Festivals as 'Mind & Body' seemed to be losing their popular support. I was reminded of Chapter Nine in SSOTBME.

To save repeating myself I must reproduce the argument as scantily as possible: that won't make it very convincing, but why should I assume that you want to be convinced?

SSOTBME

Any conscious act/thought involves a) data to be processed, b) a way of processing it.

Firstly the data: this can come from two directions, either from 'without' or from 'within'. Data from 'without' comes via the senses: I call this 'observation'. Data from 'within' comes via memory, prejudice, inspiration etc: I call this 'intuition'.

Secondly the data processing: You can link ideas logically, rationally: I call this 'logic'. Or you can link them aesthetically, quickly sensing things which 'go together' even when the logical link between them is very obscure: this process I call 'feeling'.

Two methods of input (observation and intuition) combine with two types of processing (logic and feeling) to give four kinds of thinking which I call Magical, Artistic, Religious, Scientific. Remember two things: firstly any division into just four categories must be very coarse, so do not interpret these four terms too precisely; they are very broad categories, but I still think the four words used are fairly appropriate. Secondly, all human thinking is an elaborate mixture of all elements, so these four categories really only indicate directions, like North South East West, rather than watertight compartments.

Many wondrous secrets of the universe are distilled for the enquiring reader from this simple idea in SSOTBME, and in Chapter Nine it is considered in evolutionary terms, as follows.

THE PERSONAL CYCLE

A new-born babe has very little store of memories and prejudices, so it is very much an observer, rather than intuitive. And it processes its observations by feeling rather than logic ('big soft pink things are to be sucked'). So we begin our lives as 'Magical' thinkers. By the age of 4-5 we have built up an inner world of memories which begins to overwhelm observation and shift the emphasis toward intuition, but we still have not mastered real logic. So we evolve into 'Artistic' thinking, a golden age when we live out myths of fairies and dragons and can believe in them *when we want to:* the armchair *is* a space ship when we play with it. Around 9 or so the growing sense of intuition has overwhelmed feeling and the reasoning power grows stronger. Still living off our rich inner worlds, we begin to wonder why things are as they are. This rather serious-minded phase of 'Religious' thinking lasts until after 13 when logic grows to dominate intuition, and a growing awareness of the outside world moves us into 'Scientific' thinking: 'just give me one good *reason* why I can't stay out all night,' demands the teenager.

To a rationalist the above passage is just a rather quaintly worded model of the evolution of thought through various primitive stages towards 'adult, rational thinking'. But I argue that this cycle does not stop at adolescence. I recall how my own observation grew so strong that I began to notice the flaws in scientific thought and the areas of life it could not explain away: so I inclined toward magical thinking as a student, at the age when so many of us become interested in the occult. After 23 or so we once more act out myths - the Young Man with Sports Car, the Newlyweds, etc. - until the 'saturn return' and the approaching age of 30 makes us once more seriously question our real purpose in life.

The cycle moves on - but becomes less and less clearcut, because most of us will have developed a natural bias towards one of the four directions, which tends to obscure the shifting emphasis in adult years.

THE GENERATION CYCLE

Now occult cycles tend to 'nest', like wheels within wheels: each sephiroth contains a whole tree of life, each sign contains the germ of the whole zodiac. So this cycle, which does one circuit in one generation, might lie inside a bigger cycle which runs at one quarter of the speed. Is there any evidence of this?

Let us consider the recent occult revival; did it not last for about one generation? Now I know that the real occult revival is not totally dead, something lives on, but let us isolate exactly what it is that has flared up an died away so quickly. Surely it is this: between the early sixties and the beginning of the eighties the public *got its kicks* from occultism; sensational coverage of parascience, lurid exposes of witches, books on black magic and record covers littered with occult symbolism.

But if we go back four generations (I assume about 18 years for a generation, but it might have been more like 21 years in the past) we reach the Edwardian age before the first world war. Theatre posters of that age are so rich in occult symbolism (bowls of incense, Egyptian gods etc.) that this 'art nouveau' style was actually one of the main sources of inspiration for the recent psychedelic style. This was the age when the Golden Dawn attracted public attention and so many occult orders briefly flourished.

Why this flirtation with the occult? As the previous (late Victorian) generation of theatre posters reveal a craze for public scientific demonstrations, it suggests that the Edwardian occult revival could have been a reaction against late Victorian materialism; just as the hippy generation reacted against 50s materialism. And the late Victorian public flirtation with science had followed the rise of Darwinism, and what must have looked like the fall of religion. Tracing the cycle backward I would expect to find an early Victorian 'artistic' boom (perhaps this set the style for 'Victoriana'?) and before that another occult revival. Sure enough, I find evidence that in the early 1820s fashionable society was obsessed with spiritualism.

So let us trace this apparent cycle forwards to the present. After world war one public excitement moved from magical to artistic expression, and there came the roaring twenties which saw the popularisation of so many modern art movements, an obsession with dancing and jazz, and a spate of publicity stunts like long-distance flying records, dancing marathons etc.

Out of this crazy spell the public emerged into a more serious mood. They evolved toward religious thinking for kicks, and this showed in a growing dedication to political movements: the communists, fascists and green shirts of the thirties and early forties.

After world war two, technology seemed to offer enough wonders to make the public forget politics. The Festival of Britain was a festival of technology, and this 'scientific' obsession lasted until the first sputniks, and it began to fade in the early sixties.

So, in terms of this cycle, we are in a position equivalent to the position around 1920. At the end of world war one the Luton town hall was burned down by angry ex-soldiers who had returned from the trenches to find they were unemployed, and their women had grown independent. I see some parallels; I see some differences. The punks are surely the spiritual heirs to the dadaists: those fiercely anarchic 'anti-artists' who, for example, held exhibitions of 'junk' in public lavatories. I note that so much present day pop music is monotonously dance-rhythmic, whereas ten years ago we used to sit cross-legged to *listen* to our music, and occasionally murmur such biting critical comments as 'far-out, man!' I also witness a growing tendency for record-breaking stunts as a route to fleeting fame.

On the strength of this slender evidence, dare I make predictions? Of course not! Oh, what the hell, here goes....

PREDICTIONS

First question: Does this mean the end of occultism? Was the whole magical revival a mere passing fad? Not at all. When we reacted against 50s materialism we did not throw away our transistor radios, we were merely less inclined to show them off. There was surely more widespread technology about in 1970 than in 1950; more electronics in our music, more portable radios and so on. But we *used* these gadgets (sometimes a little coyly) rather than raved about them, as we would have in the 'super-sonic, ultra-midget jet-propelled' days of the fifties.

Now I do not really believe that the 'great occult explosion' we have witnessed has really given birth to many great adepts as yet. It was mostly a lot of froth. In 1970 the general public attitude was to get frightfully excited if you met someone who 'actually practiced witchcraft'; to talk for ages about 'mysterious psychic powers'; and to be proud to believe there might 'really be something in astrology'. I can see the time coming shortly when people will discover than many of their acquaintances *are* witches, actually *practice yoga* for fifteen minutes a day, or have the gift of recognising astrological types, but that they 'never bothered to mention the fact'. Occultism will be practiced, rather than talked about.

So my first prediction for the 80s is that sales of occult books will not recover, but that the books bought will be rather better used than those bought in the recent past. Occultism will become a rather more everyday matter.

Secondly, what about this revival of fascination with the arts? There should be a growth of new movements in the arts if the cycle runs true to form. Now I find this very interesting, because it is all too easy to believe that there can be nothing left in the way of artistic expression that was not tried out in the 1920s. So what *could* be totally new?

Let us consider new art *forms* rather than movements. Two totally new art forms emerged into the thirties: radio and cinema. There has not been any other really new art form since. (TV is only really mini-radiocinema, whatever its fans try to claim for it, and electronic music also dates from the earlier era). At the end of world war one both film and radio were, to the general public, little more than technical diversions for low-brow amusement. By the beginning of the thirties it was possible to go to the cinema for a profoundly moving experience, and radio serials could keep families on tenterhooks for night after night. Two great new art forms had come of age.

Now I can immediately think of one 1980s technical diversion that is far from being Great Art: video games are in their infancy.

Video games bore me to death, but I see potential. Dungeons & Dragons is an attempt to lead the soul on a mystery quest, an initiatory journey akin to that trod by the celebrants at Eleusis. But it is so crude.

The essential difference between video games and television lies in the vital ingredient of spectator interaction. That is why they could claim to be a totally new art form, where television could not. When this interaction grows more subtle, amazing possibilities could emerge.

Imagine a video game machine which could make judgments about the person playing it, based upon such considerations as a) how fast he reacts to different stimuli, b) how boldly or tentatively he pushes the buttons, c) changing skin resistance as certain words or situations are presented on the screen, d) freudian slips etc. Such a machine could present a tailor-made series of ordeals that would amount of an initiatory journey for each individual player. The trouble with present-day occult initiation is the cynical realisation that the adept at whose feet you sit is probably only human, all too human: how would you feel about a machine that can analyse you in minutes and outwit you at every turn?

I predict that by the year 2000 we will be able to come out of a games arcade with tears on our cheeks, souls in a turmoil of wonderment, - every bit as profound and fruitful as the wonderment engendered by a great film or play.

Third question, and I've kept the most lurid one to the end, what are the prospects for 'over the top' occultism?

The recent revival of occultism owed a lot to those sensible, down-to-earth occultists who showed the public that we were not all crazy. The essence of the typical positive magazine article on the occult ten years ago was as follows: *'I was so surprised to find that in my quiet little neighbourhood there should actually be a group of people who took an interest in these weird ideas, that it took me some time to pluck up courage to go along to one of their meetings. There I had my second surprise: far from being a bunch of wild-eyed whackos they were all really nice down-to-earth people from all walks of life: a teacher, a computer salesman, a bank clerk, a psychologist, three housewives. And I heard more straight commonsense being spoken in that group than I'd heard for a longtime elsewhere'.*

Yes, occultism earned respect because decent occultists publicly divorced themselves from 'those lunatics that give occultism a bad name'; yet this repeated denial of those lunatics is now in danger of becoming a mechanical catch phrase. By playing so safe, are we perhaps throwing away too much?

Here follows an outrageous invocation: 'O ye big, hairy, wild-eyed mega-thelemites of 1973, all ye sons and reincarnations of the Beast, come back, for All is forgiven!'

How dare I perpetrate this outrage? Because I argue thus: granted that 99% of those mega-thelemites might have been mere empty shells of ego inflation being born aloft on the spume of public sensationalism, then they will never answer my invocation anyway; because they will simply collapse before the laughter of the rather more cynical public of the 80s. On the other hand if some bearded, becloaked and wild eyed being does storm into the public arena with a fusillade of smoke bombs and a twirling of magic wands, calling itself the Antichrist, claiming to know the secrets of the universe (and being prepared to sell them for some extortionate sum of money) then my immediate 1983 reaction might not be 'that lunatic is giving occultism a bad name' but rather 'Wow! I admire such courage'.

I can see the progression of public crazes from science, through magic, to art in these terms: a person grows weary of the stolid know-all-the-answers certainties of rationalism; nervously he approaches magic in search of the miraculous. Relief! his fears were unfounded! Magic is not madness; he finds an acceptable alternative to rationalism but, alas, the very sensibleness of magic eventually begins to pall; perhaps it was madness that was really wanted all along? So we progress into the artistic craze and it lasts until a growing sense of guilt, or something, leads us out of it. In these terms the 'over the top' magician could have a real place in the 1980s.

Consider again the transition from Edwardian occultism to the roaring 20s. Some time after writing the Book of the Law, Aleister Crowley decided to give up magic and to concentrate his attention on poetry, mountain climbing and such pursuits. But in the 20s he re-emerged to fame as the 'wickedest man in the world'. How much was his own innate degeneracy, as his detractors would have it, and how much was a genuine response to the need of the age?

It does not just take courage to go 'over the top', it takes humility. Recently Ramsey Dukes, in financial straits, saw Jupiter and Venus about to bestow their generous favours upon certain sensitive points of his horoscope. So he made a pact with Fate and filled in a football pool coupon, saying 'make me a pools millionaire and I will buy a mansion, fill it with weirdies, devise a 'heavy metal' magical philosophy to make Kenneth Grant read like Beatrix Potter, and announce myself as he Antichrist.' Fate, with a remarkable show of good taste, walked by and left Ramsey Dukes in financial straits. Ramsey reckons that was because of his unconquered ego: amongst all the glare of publicity, the scandal, the outrage and the money, Ramsey would not have been able to resist the temptation of letting out the fact that, beneath it all, he was still basically quite a nice person. In fact Ramsey was not prepared to sacrifice All for the Cause. Raspberries on toast.

So that is my third prediction: although the mainstay of occultism in the 80s is going to be very practical and 'unexciting', there will be a definite place open for a small but very intense brand of 'over the top' magic. *(With 90s hindsight, I would link the recent satanism hysteria to this prediction, Editor)*

AQUARIAN AGE

Now I have written at length about a fleeting human cycle of merely 75 years duration. In view of our high expectations of the occult revival in 1970, does this mean I have made a mockery of the Age of Aquarius?

If you believe that wearing a kaftan, smoking dope while sitting cross legged and saying 'far out man' is truly the be-all of the Age of Aquarius then I would agree that in 1982 the last remains of the Age of Aquarius were finally scraped off the greasy plate of public adulation into the pedal bin of history. (Don't be misled by this cynicism: I do think that the hippy craze was very important. What I am saying is that it was 'eighteen years' important, not 'two thousand years' important.)

But if you can recognise those facets of the occult revival which are merely transitory and, having isolated them, can turn to see what remains, then a very different picture emerges. We have looked at the SSOTBME cycle at the human level, let us now look at it at a slower, cosmic level and see if Ramsey can flog a little more juice out of his poor, hard-pressed theories. Faster moving cycles are more fun, but the soul does yearn for more depth.

What happened to the Age of Aquarius? Around 1970 it was very tempting to equate the coming of the Age of Aquarius with the flourishing hippy movement. The trouble with so doing is that the waning of the hippy movement then suggests the waning of the Age of Aquarius.

Personally I feel that people expect too much too fast of the Age of Aquarius, and I predict that most of us will go to our graves still not knowing what its significance will be, or whether it has 'really begun'. In the first part of this essay I argued that the hippy movement was not so a symptom of the 2000 year Age of Aquarius, as an 18-20 year generational effect: a much more fleeting and trivial cycle, but still one well worth considering simply because it was much more immediate and relevant to everyday affairs. It arose from considering the SSOTBME model in a personal, human evolutionary context.

Before saying any more about historical cycles I should point out that my emphasis on cycles is not meant to deny a progressive view of history. A spiral of evolution is a useful concept, and such a spiral (or helical) motion can be analysed as the sum of a linear (progressive) and circular (cyclic) motion. My concentration on the cycles could help us to recognise them for what they are, and perhaps therefore make it easier in the long run to recognise true progress where it exists.

THE COSMIC CYCLES

My cycle of about 75 years was made up of 4 generations of about 18 years. It was a cycle based on a 'human' timescale. But a 2000 year Age of Aquarius exists not on a human, but on a 'cosmic' level. If the SSOTBME cycle is relevant to that level, then which of the four states is most appropriate to the Age of Aquarius: Religion, Science, Magic or Art?

Those of us too heavily programmed to equate the Age of

Aquarius with the events around 1970 might jump to reply 'Magic', but I would not agree. The air signs are traditionally associated with logical reasoning, and the equinoctial precession through Aquarius to Capricorn, i.e., through Air to Earth, is very suggestive of the SSOTBME cycle progression from logic to observation through the 'Science' sector. Uranus, the ruler of Aquarius, is also ruler of science, invention, electronics, etc. I know there is a traditional attribution of 'Uranus the Magician', but surely that is more a reference to the 'magic of science' or the working of wonders than to truly magical working. So I would expect the Scientific spirit to rule the Age of Aquarius. In this case the previous age would have been ruled by the Religious spirit - is this true? I think there can be little doubt as to this. The last two thousand years have been dominated by what I called the 'Religious' spirit - whether in the form of religion per se, or in the form of strong political conviction. Religion has been taken very seriously, to an extent that makes the religions of the pre-christian era seem comparatively frivolous. Most of the wars of the Age of Pisces have been fought from a basically religious or political motivation.

By contrast it is easy to believe that wars of the two thousand years before the Age of Pisces were fought not so much for religious reasons as for greed. There is a definite impression in that era of one nation becoming fascinated by another nation's culture, and its treasures, and going to war in order to gain those treasures. Certainly the Romans were fascinated by the Greek culture, and Alexander's conquests are popularly associated with his collection of all the wisdom of the world into the great library he founded. So I suggest that, true to the model described earlier, the phase that precedes the Religious phase is the 'Artistic' phase. The two thousand years before Christ were ruled by the Artistic spirit, the last two thousand years have been ruled by the Religious spirit, and the Age of Aquarius is due to be ruled by the Scientific spirit.

If the Age of Aquarius really is to be the Age of Science in these terms, how has it come to be associated so strongly with the occult revival? As when we considered the Personal and the Generational cycles I think the answer lies in the nested cycle that makes one complete circle in each two thousand year age: a cycle made up to four periods of five hundred years.

For the last five hundred years the dominant philosophy has been the rationalist philosophy that I attribute to the Science sector in the diagram. Since the sixteenth century the earlier Religious ideas have been on the retreat, in the face of the progress made by Scientific philosophy.

It is tempting to flatter ourselves into believing that this rational philosophy is a brand new invention without precedent among our primitive ancestors, who were willing to bow down and worship just about anything it seems. So it is surprising to find that the same sceptical, rational philosophy was dominant two thousand years ago. In China at the time writers were making a mockery of divination and astrology, using just the same sort of arguments that Patrick Moore would use today. It has been suggested that only their clumsy numerical system held the Greeks back from developing practical steam engines before the birth of Christ. And although rationalists like to think of alchemy as a primitive superstition that gave birth to 'real' chemistry, it must be remembered that alchemy itself grew out of the very highly developed metallurgical technology of the pre-Christian arabs.

What I am suggesting is that the rational Scientific philosophy held a dominant position in the five centuries before Christ which was similar to its position in the last five hundred years. But, far from marking an endpoint in human evolution, this Scientific philosophy evolved into, or gave way to, a Magical philosophy of the Dark Ages that spanned the next five centuries. These were the centuries when the church was struggling against Gnostic, Neoplatonic and other magical philosophies. The following five centuries, until the year 1000 AD, bear the imprint of an Artistic philosophy: this was the age of Chivalry, the age of King Arthur and the age in which most fairy tales are set. Then from the eleventh to the sixteenth century Religious philosophy ruled men's minds.

In this way we see that within the Age of Pisces we have passed through four philosophical stages (readers with a better knowledge of history than myself will see from my cavalier use of historical generalisations that this is a 'woolly theory' that I am creating, but they need not dismiss it for that reason: when the wind of change blows cold, nothing is more comforting than a woolly theory, so long as it does not have too many holes in it.) But even though Magic, Art, Religion and Science have each taken turns to dominate man's thinking, it is the Religious spirit that has held the reins of power - a manifestation of the Religious spirit.

In these terms the initial passage into the Age of Aquarius would be marked by two changes that might at first seem contradictory: a shift from the Religious spirit of the Age of Pisces to the Scientific spirit of the Age of Aquarius, coupled with a growth of Magical philosophy in place of the Scientific philosophy of the last five centuries. To resolve the apparent contradiction I will give some examples of how this might happen.

SCIENCE INTO MAGIC

Consider the Arabic metallurgy that evolved into alchemy. Before the birth of Christ it was a straightforward, unmystical technology and it flourished thanks to the open minded, freely communicating rational philosophy of that time, and also thanks to its valuable application to the coining of metal currency and the protection against counterfeiters. But around the time of Christ this technology became increasingly cloaked in secrecy. It seems that the rulers for whom the metallurgists worked felt driven by greed (typical of the Artistic spirit of the old Age of Aries) and desire for political power (contributed by the Religious spirit of the new Age of Pisces) into hushing up the technologists and forcing them to work in secret. But the Scientific method depends upon a free exchange of information; when this is forbidden it begins to develop Magical tendencies. Cloaked in secrecy and coded in symbols, Arabic science evolved into Alchemy.

Now I can see a similar tendency in modern science. It has grown so useful that, as before, it is in danger of becoming muffled. As before we have the repressive effect of political power (thanks to the remnant of the Religious spirit of the Age of Pisces) which tries to imprison scientists into secret establishments - this is not only done by national governments, it is also practiced by commercial combines - but curiously enough the coming rulership of the Age of Aquarius by the Scientific spirit is also contributing to this decline. This is because science has been encouraged to grow so fast that it becomes the victim of its own divisive, fragmenting tendencies. Even when not repressed, scientists find it increasingly difficult to communicate with each other simply because their work has become so specialised. This fragmentation and isolation sets the stage for the decline of Science and the growth of Magic.

Traditionally, any unusual scientific discoveries, or controversial experimental results produced in obscure laboratories, have usually been published and have either been accepted by the scientific fraternity or else (as so happens in the case of parascience) they have proved unacceptable elsewhere and have therefore been discredited. This process of free communication has tended to sift out anomalies and preserve the purity of accepted scientific fact. But if this process is frustrated, so that future scientists will be working in ever greater isolation, then curious mutations of accepted scientific fact will no longer be automatically aborted. Research workers in secret defence laboratories, who find they can detect enemy submarines with a dowsing rod, will *go on* being able to detect them in this way; and will learn to develop and extend this skill, shielded from the common scepticism of the scientific fraternity. (No doubt they will eventually get round to fasting, burning incense and invoking appropriate deities to sharpen their sensitivity!)

Another route by which Science could evolve into Magic lies along the increasing dependence upon statistical evidence as ever soggier 'soft sciences' are evolved. As explained in SSOTBME, once you start to make predictions upon a basis of previous statistical correlation alone - without constructing any theoretical causal framework - then you are being no more scientific than an astrologer who learns to interpret charts from experience. This is true however impressive sounding are the figures quoted.

Similarly the advertising agency that offers to replace your 'haphazard, unprofessional approach' with an 'up-to-the-minute, scientific promotional strategy' and does so by giving your brand name a 'new image' to 'optimize positive consumer reaction'; by suggesting a fresh new colour scheme based on bright tints with 'proven high stimulus response'; by littering your adverts with trendy imagery in order to 'redefine the catchment category by maximizing appeal at a lower socio-econmic band'; this advertising agency, for all its fancy pseudo-scientific jargon, is simply invoking Mercury to help your business to prosper.

But the interesting point is that, in none of these three examples does anyone actually *admit* to doing Magic, nor even allow themselves to believe in such nonsense! Why is this? I suggest that this is a symptom of the presiding Scientific spirit of the new age: just as the Magic of the Age of Pisces was so often safely cloaked in the mantle of Religion, or Religious terminology, so will the accepted magic of the Age of Aquarius be ever wrapped in pseudo-scientific jargon.

As a matter of interest on this score, when I suggested that in the Age of Aries major wars were fought in the 'Artistic' spirit of cultural take-over bids, and in the Age of Pisces major wars were fought on 'Religious' grounds; we would then expect wars in the coming Age of Aquarius to be fought on 'Scientific' grounds! Does this mean that the trend-setting war for the coming age was the Spanish Civil War, when the Nazis apparently entered the war not so much for political commitment as in order to try out their new weapons? And is this why, although we now publicly praise our heroic veterans of the Falklands, at the time of the conflict there was actually more talk about how well our previously untried *weapons* were performing in the field? *(The recent Gulf War carried this even further, Editor)* How long will the public put up with the omnipresent uncertainty as to whether the world would survive a nuclear war until, in despair, it demands that the question be resolved in a practical test? In other words, might not the next world war be less of an ideological struggle but rather more of an experiment in response to a group need to generate a catastrophe in a world too heavily policed to allow for any minor revolutions?

SUMMARY

In this essay I have looked at the trends accompanying the transition into the Age of Aquarius, and I have isolated three separate cyclic phenomena. Whether this has clarified the question, or merely confused it is up to the individual to decide. I feel that it has at least resolved some paradoxes.

For one thing I was never totally happy with the idea that came across in, for example, the musical 'Hair'; the idea that the Age of Aquarius was an age of groovy, turned on, zonked out, free spirited Love. This hardly lined up with my idea of the astrological sign of Aquarius as a fixed air sign (in fact it sounded rather more like the ideal of Pisces than the clear, detached Aquarian ideal!). The passing of the hippy era does not by any means mean that it was a trivial fashion, but it does suggest that it was not essentially linked to the Age of Aquarius. My discussion of the Generational Cycle puts the hippy revolution in its place - without trivialising it in the way loved by cynical journalists.

The Uri Geller craze has abated, but still we see a steady evolution towards Magical thinking in the sciences - how does this fit in with the Age of Aquarius? My 'philosophical' cycle of four periods of five centuries each would fit this apparent progression from Science into Magic.

But why is it that we occultists are nevertheless denied the satisfaction of seeing our subject granted official recognition? I suggest that this is due to the Scientific spirit of the Age of Aquarius, which will ensure that the name of Science is ever revered, and that in coming centuries occult movements will remain as 'underground' movements except when disguised in scientific jargon (e.g. Scientology). The same will be true of Religious movements: I suspect they in turn will need to justify their 'psychological validity' if they are to be officially recognised.

The trouble with this essay is that I am ignorant of history and have made sweeping assumptions. Would a careful study of history reinforce these ideas or would it disprove them? Alternatively, was my ignorance a necessary condition for clairvoyance?

"Farewell to Synthesis" from The Golden Hind Vol I No 3 by trickster - magus and master of illusions Austin Osman Spare.

10 - THE CHARLATAN AND THE MAGUS

First published in The Lamp of Thoth

This essay was written for reading out at a meeting of The Society, London, in Spring 1984, hence its "lecture" style and hence the references to Ellic Howe, who was also a member of The Society and who had been investigating the history of the OTO in the same critical spirit as in his book about the Golden Dawn.

It remains my favourite essay, and its theme is still dear to my heart.

Recently a friend read me a draft chapter of a novel he was writing. It was a novel of a spiritual quest, and in this chapter there was a chance encounter of the hero and a group of bohemian extroverts at a cafe table: they joined up for a meal and some wine together, and this encounter was later destined to lead to the next clue in the hero's search.

I was asked for comment on the chapter, and one comment that I made has since haunted me. I asked if this encounter was a truly important signpost upon the hero's spiritual highway. It was. In that case my suggestion was that, at the end of their meal together, the group should find themselves slightly short of cash, to the effect that the hero then felt obliged to foot the remainder of the bill.

Why did this seem right? Why did literary aesthetics seem to require that an important step on the spiritual path be marked by an element of roguery? not so much an out and out swindle that would have turned the hero away in disgust, but rather just that streak of caddishness that would allow the group to order more wine than they could afford, on the strength of an unconscious calculation of the hero's assets and his sense of generosity, or even his fear of unpleasantness?

Why is it right that an important spiritual turning point should be just sufficiently tainted, as to give the hero reason to pause before stepping forward? For might he not well have spent the evening fuming that he had been conned into paying the drinks, and decided to have no more to do with his new-found acquaintances? and might he not as a result have missed his chance?

If I sense that spiritual diamonds should always come with a bit of muck upon them, am I only reflecting a cynical lesson that my own inadequate life has forced upon me, or am I in fact tuning in to a vital cosmic principle?

For a start: was this idea of mine a purely personal aberration? My first evidence to the contrary is that the author agreed with my suggestion, and proceeded to write it into his next draft.

The subject of this essay is literally a tricky one. Normally I do not like to write about a subject until my views on it are in some sense complete and "buttoned up". In the case of the Charlatan and the Magus I am writing on a topic that has haunted me for many years, but which is far from being clarified. Indeed I will be asking more questions than giving real answers. You may even miss the point of what I am saying, and wonder if I am simply pulling your legs.

Perhaps this is an inevitable consequence of my subject: perhaps it is right that I should assume the mantle of the Trickster in trying to write about the Trickster?

There is, however, one problem that I can anticipate: a problem best described by analogy. Look at the behaviour of this pendulum...

[*at this point the speaker produced a pendulum, made from a thin rod with a bar magnet on the bottom end, and allowed it to oscillate in the magnetic field of a powerful magnet placed on the table top*]

... Notice how its motion is deflected because of opposing magnetic poles.

The demonstration I really wanted to show you was rather less portable: it was of a billiard table with a slight dip in its surface. A ball rolling across that table and towards that dip would be deflected in a similar fashion to the pendulum. But in this case the motion could be more easily looked at in two different ways. From our point of view, as outside observers, the ball has been very obviously been deflected from the straight and narrow under the influence of forces connected with the distortion of the table's surface. However we can instead put ourselves imaginatively in the ball's position, and argue that there has been no deflection. For the definition of a straight line on a billiard table is that it is the path a ball will roll along unless some outside force acts upon it. The ball knows only the two dimensions of the table's surface, it does not have our superior knowledge of the third dimension, and the fact that the surface is warped in that dimension. So, as far as the ball is concerned, it has simply rolled along a straight line.

This relativistic argument can be adapted to the demonstration of the pendulum: on the one hand we, as outside observers, can argue that we have seen a pendulum being deflected by a magnetic force; on the other hand we could imagine that the pendulum has simply continued upon what *it* thinks is a straight line, because it does not realise that its local universe has been distorted by a strong magnetic field.

The analogy that I wish to suggest is this: that just as the pendulum's field of movement can be locally distorted by a powerfully charged magnet, so also can a human's field of reason be distorted by a powerfully charged concept. And in the vicinity of that concept reason can run along a path that appears warped to an outside observer, yet appears perfectly straight to the thinker.

Consider a theologian of a past age listening to a brilliant discourse upon the nature of angels. He is no idiot, he uses his full knowledge and powers of logic to analyse what is said, and he is very impressed. That is, until a chance remark exposes the speaker to be a protestant heretic. Suddenly his whole discourse is so suspect as to be worthless. As outsiders to a world so heavily charged with concepts of godliness and heresy, we see that the listener has been deflected through a complete U-turn as soon as he approached the realisation that the speaker was a heretic.

As outsiders we see a U-turn. But what if we were part of that theologian's world? Would we be able to provide a logical explanation as to why the speaker's being a heretic means that he incapable of saying anything worthwhile about angels? In other words would we be able to describe the forces that deflected the theologian's reason? Or would we take his reaction so much for granted, that we would refuse to recognise that his reason *had* done a U-turn?

Do you see the problem?

Well, consider a more contemporary example. The famous scientist who decides to investigate the paranormal and so arranges a laboratory seance with Minny Blenkinsop the Flower medium who is at present the big name amongst spiritualists because of her amazing ability to materialise flowers from the spirit world. The scientist, after several interesting experiments, catches Minny smuggling a bunch of violets into the laboratory in her bloomers. He abandons the experiments forthwith.

I wonder if, in some future age, we might not judge the scientist's dismissal of the fraudulent medium to be just as arbitrary as the theologian's dismissal of the heretic? Could our attitudes change to that extent? or is mankind doomed to lose its apparent ability to make endless fun of its ancestors?

In SSOTBME I argued that Good versus Evil was the dominant concept of the Age of Pisces, because the spirit of that age was the religious spirit. And I predicted that the dominant concept of the Age of Aquarius would be Truth versus Illusion. Now I would like to revise my opinion. Good versus Evil is always the most heavily charged concept in men's minds: the difference is that in the Piscean age ''Good'' = ''God'' and ''Evil'' = ''the Devil'', while in the new age ''Good'' = ''Truth'' and ''Evil'' = ''Illusion''.

So, when in this essay I attempt to turn our attention to the very nature of illusion and our response to it, I am attempting something that makes great demands upon my audience. And I will need to return again and again to this analogy. If, instead of averting our gaze in disgust, we turn to face the Charlatan, then we are doing the psychological equivalent of a physical investigation in the vicinity of a Black Hole.

Who are the great occult figures of this century? Blavatsky, Steiner, Besant, Crowley, Gurdjieff, Rajneesh... Those present might add names like Mathers and Westcott to the list; the layman might add Uri Geller and some of the recent gurus from the East. But is there a single name that is untainted by the smell of charlatanry?

Whether it is actual fraud - as in Blavatsky's faked spiritual phenomena, the holy dust of a recent guru, or the forged cipher manuscripts of the Golden Dawn - or whether it is sheer roguery - as in the life of Crowley or Gurdjieff - or whether it is a most unspiritual aptitude for making easy money - as in most gurus from the East: whatever form it takes I defy anyone to find a stainless saint among occult leaders. Even the impeccable Krishnamurti was created out of scandal. And Lemuel Johnstone didn't even have the decency to exist.

This is the problem that has haunted me for so long. So let us examine it straightaway in the light of my analogy. How did you react to my observation about the occult leaders? There are two standardised reactions.

The first is to think ''well of course they were all charlatans. That is all occultism is: just a great big con game''. This is the sceptic's response.

The second is to think "oh, hell, not another debunking essay". This is the reaction of the defensive believer.

A third reaction, the reaction of the committed believer, is to think, for example, "he's quite right about all those other cranks, but surely he has heard that those stories about Madame Blavatsky were merely trumped-up charges..." and then to regurgitate a mass of evidence that other historians seem to have overlooked. Or to argue that "he is right about all those second- rate masters, but doesn't he realise that Crowley was simply wise enough to understand people and to know what compromises are necessary when dealing with the masses..." and to go on with a most ingenious argument that does not quite fit all the facts.

All three responses, are liable to totally colour your whole attitude to this subject. Each reaction amounts to a deflection from the straight path. All three are so natural that I cannot yet ask you to resist them, all I ask is that you pause a moment to think which response is nearest to your own. To be conscious of your inclination is the first step towards independence.

What sort of independence might we hope to gain?

In Anita Mason's novel about Simon Magus there is a lovely portrayal of the rational mentality struggling to adapt to a world that was slipping into magical thinking. I have argued elsewhere (SSOTBME and the previous essay) that we are at present witnessing a transformation from an era of basically rational to an era of basically magical thinking, and that the last time that this happened was around the birth of Christ - the difference being that last time it all happened in the name of religion, while this time it is happening in the name of science.

In The Illusionist we are at one point lead through the mental contortions that lead to one character becoming able to say "I believe because it is absurd". This is done too convincingly to be summarised here.

The point is this: how many of us would be able to do the equivalent? When you discover that your favourite guru has got feet of clay, the natural reaction is either to deny the evidence, or to desert your guru in anger or contempt. How many of us could say "I follow him *because* he is a charlatan?"

But how ridiculous! I have overstated my case, gone too far

too soon. I have taken you too close to that black hole, and now perhaps you are wondering if this essay is a spoof! Some careful repair work needs to be done.

Consider the psychical researcher, one of Freud's circle described in J. Webb's The Occult Establishment, who abandons experiments with a promising medium when he catches her cheating. This attitude is so normal as to demand no justification. But will it always be so? Since pondering this problem I have begun to find such behaviour increasingly peculiar.

Consider instead the upright citizen, president of the local Round Table, Chairman of the local school's Board of Governors, and so on. He has three children, a mock tudor house and a happy marriage. Then he finds that his wife is cheating on him. What does he do? If his shame is so great that he at once arranges for a divorce, or even leaves for another job in another part of the country, we would say that he has over-reacted. By the standards of today he is trying to live out an absurdly unrealistic ideal of perfection. And yet a century ago such action would seem too normal to need any justification. Why was it accepted? I think that even today we would find such a rigid code very powerful in the outer world: such behaviour would impress society by its sheer audacity, and such a man would have a good chance of reaching the sort of social heights described. But what we would also recognise is that such behaviour is vastly less productive in the more "inner" world of human relationships. The man would end up as a very lonely success story, because he refused to face the world as it really is. As my good friend The Hon. Hugo C. St.J. l'Estrange said on the occasion of his first divorce, at a time when the society columns were dragging his name through the mire: "when will mankind grow out of its flirtation with Christian ethics, and face the fact that the Great Cosmic Principle is not to do what is right and honourable, but to do what is wrong in *style*."

So what of the scientific researcher who approaches the universe with such cleanliness and honour that the first hint of trickery is often the end of the matter? As in the last example, this attitude has resulted in considerable successes, does this mean that we should therefore admit that it is proven? or is this very success an obstacle to further progress? Might we not grow out of this scrupulous approach and find, as in the last example, that although the puritan approach may have great power in the outer world, such behaviour is much less productive in the more ''inner'' world of spiritual development. Is the rationalist approach to the occult also destined to lead to a lonely loss of contact with the world as it is?

''But that is an unfair comparison'' says the researcher, ''for the medium's reliability is *central* to what I am investigating, whereas that wife's reliability is a side issue.'' Try telling that to the man who once stood beside his wife and shared vows at the altar!

Yes, I really mean it. I really am suggesting that perhaps there is a fundamental limitation in the rational approach. Not just a slight practical limitation, but a fundamental one.

Too often we approach the occult in the same scrupulous spirit. Because we believe in an absolute truth, we set our sights on it and are in danger of missing the reality.

I am sure that, in terms of sheer numbers, the majority of mankind probably subscribes to some religion that insists that the world is an illusion; even our own scientists are increasingly making it seem like an illusion. And yet, when we want to find out about the world, so many of us still choose to seek the answers among those who search for absolute truth. Might you not find out more about the nature of an illusion by following those who deal with illusions? Might not the spiritual path lead through the world of mountebanks and charlatans, rather than away from it?

Consider the tarot pack. The 22 trumps are often spoken of as symbolising the path of spiritual progress. So does the series start with a High Priest? or the authority of an Emperor? No, it begins with a Fool dressed in rags, and the next card is of a Juggler or common street magician (at least until recent packs improved his image a bit).

Another example. Imagine that for some reason, (perhaps because you are on the run from the secret service) you find yourself forced to start a new life as an unknown stranger in a some big city's slums, or even worse in some South American or Far East shanty town. You have nothing but the clothes you stand up in, however you do have an offer of help. Two offers to be precise. The first offer comes from the very learned Professor

Wiesenstein of Edinburgh University. He offers to put his entire sociological and psychological researches at your disposal, including his brilliant papers on "Emerging Social Structures in the South American Shanty Town", on "The Psychology of Aggression in the Urban Underworld" and so on. The other offer comes from Rico The Razor, a small-time pimp and petty crook, who says "Stick wiv me, mate, n'I'll show yer around".

Somehow you know that both offers are equally sincere, but that you may only accept one of them. What I am suggesting is that Rico's offer should be given serious consideration.

So often the artist who thinks deeply about the world, finds himself drawn to the fairground and the circus for his inspiration. Might not we too take our eyes away from the dream of the Magus, and take another look at the Charlatan? The moment that this bold decision is taken, you hit difficulties. Don't panic! As any seeker knows, if the way is hard it is probably the right way. You see, as long as you were seeking a Magus, you found only a world full of Charlatans. But now that you set out to find a real, wholehearted occult charlatan, you discover that they are all so bloody high-minded.

Again, is it my own craziness, or am I right in feeling that this very fact is a vital clue that we are on the right path? If the transition from charlatan to magus can be so swift, does it not confirm that we are living out our inner states, that the world is illusion and we are getting closer to the Master of Illusions? Woops, again I've gone ahead too fast!

So where do we seek the charlatan? In my search I decided to take a tip from the second trump of the Tarot pack, and become an associate of the Magic Circle.

First I went to the public library to read some recent books on conjuring. One observation struck me at once: the number of conjurors who felt that their art was going through a lean phase at present. Some blamed this on television.

Only in one book was the problem discussed at greater length: "Entertaining With ESP" by Doc Shiels. Doc suggested that the reason that conjuring no longer draws the crowds, is that the public now knows too well that it is all just trickery. Nobody is naive enough to believe in magic anymore. One hundred years ago, although few people really thought you could create a rabbit in a hat, there was at least a belief in the mysterious wisdom of the east, that could create amazing hypnotic illusions. And there was also the chance of some unknown inventor creating a scientific miracle in his back room (without The Military swooping in to claim it). In other words there was just the slightest streak of public openness to the miraculous. And this made conjuring great. To support his theory he pointed out that there was one area of conjuring that was still as healthy as ever: namely mentalism, or the art of faking extra-sensory perception. He suggested that the strength of mentalism lay in the fact that this was one area of magic where the public still had that streak of belief: perhaps telepathy *is* possible? In this respect it was suggested that conjurors had been their own worst enemies: by trying so hard to dissociate themselves from the fake spiritualists, they had lost their roots in the public imagination. They had become too scrupulous.

Sure enough, I found that most conjurors are pathetically scrupulous. I even witnessed mentalists who began their act not with a lecture on the mysterious powers of the human mind, but with a sort of disclaimer to the effect that they claimed no superior powers, and that the act we were about to see would be performed merely by ingenious trickery. The effect was about as appetising as an EEC regulation ingredients list on a sauce bottle. What the man was saying was that his act would not present any challenge to the spectators, except that of trying to guess how it was done. We were to be presented with a series of puzzles.

The trouble is this: we all enjoy a book of puzzles, but etiquette demands that the answers should appear in the back of the book. Here was a set of puzzles devoid of such relief - for conjurors are not only scrupulous about occult disclaimers, they are also scrupulous about keeping their secrets.

This was to me a sound reason why the public image of the conjuror seems to be more that of an irritant, than of a significant artist. Perhaps you are so used to the image of the conjuror as the man in the loud jacket who does clever things against tasteless background of feeble jokes, that you cannot see why I should expect conjuring to be significant? But if you think about it, isn't conjuring a most amazing concept? The art of creating apparent impossibility, the purest manipulation of illusion; were it not such a red herring I would be tempted to divert into an argument that this playing with illusion was in fact the original source of ALL art.

I also found the greatest intensity of anti-occult scepticism amongst conjurors. Uri Geller was despised with an anger that reeked of jealousy: "How could the public rush to see such a pathetic magic demonstration, when your average conjuring professional can barely scrape a living?" To me the answer seemed obvious.

Uri Geller did not become famous for providing an amusing evening's diversion; he became famous for having opened a crack in the public's sense of reality. For a year there was a new topic of conversation in the public bar, people began to look at the world and wonder about it. In terms of quantity, if not quality, he was probably the greatest stimulus to popular philosophising since Einstein. Yet these conjurors were blind to his real achievement, seeing only details of poor technique. When this close inspection provided no explanation of Geller's success, they resorted to the old explanatory scapegoat: public gullibility.

So much for the Magic Circle as a hotbed of charlatans: instead of finding Geller's disciples I found his detractors. But in the library there was a most interesting type of book: anonymous books with titles like "The Confessions of a Medium". These books are rather crudely written accounts of how to be a fake psychic. They describe ways of picking up clues from a person's appearance, mannerisms and clothing, and how to use those clues to colour a few generalised statements that are designed to sound-out the client's problems. Step by step the client is milked for information, while the medium is apparently uttering great wisdom; then these facts are finally revealed to the astonished client - who goes away to tell the world about the medium's amazing psychic gift.

Why were these books kept in the library? and why indeed are such books ready sellers in the scrupulously honest world of conjuring? I have only heard them recommended as "giving useful hints on the presentation of a mental act" - but anyone who starts such an act by disclaiming all occult powers has certainly not learned his techniques from these sources!

My guess is that these books are wonderfully reassuring to the opponents of the occult, and that is why they are popular. Read them, and you will never again be impressed by a clairvoyant; when astonished friends tell stories of great psychics they have met, you will respond with a knowing smile. These books, written by the very people who made a living out of faking clairvoyance, are the ultimate defense against a belief in the paranormal.... except for one curious anomaly.

Before I unveil that anomaly, and while you are all trembling on the edgesof your seats, may I remind you of my pendulum analogy?

What do you think so far? Has my revolutionary thesis shattered your world? are you fuming at my affrontery? You are much more likely to be thinking along these lines: "Of course he is basically right, unless you are prepared to face up to the worst, you will never really get to the roots of the human condition. Nobody should expect any guru to be utterly perfect. And I suppose that parascientists might lose worthwhile evidence if they make absolutely no allowance for human weakness."

If that is what you think my essay is getting at, then too late! You have passed the danger zone and already been deflected. Try harder next time and meanwhile here are some more clues as to what to look for.

Nothing in that version of my thesis was at all revolutionary: it made this essay no more than a plea for tolerance. Am I suggesting that parascientists, instead of dismissing their subjects at the first sign of fraud, should learn to swallow their pride, breath a heavy sigh, give a little lecture on honesty and the principle of objective scientific truth... then allow the experiments to continue under slightly stricter controls? Would that be revolutionary? No: I suspect that parascientists have already adopted some such approach. Is it progress? No, not *real* progress.

Imagine that you are the errant wife of that respectable citizen I described. But, instead of being faced with instant divorce and banishment, you find that your so-perfect husband is prepared to brace himself against his public disgrace, and is willing to give you a little lecture and a second chance to prove yourself. Is this progress? Perhaps you might at first feel relieved and penitent, but wouldn't you come to see this patronising generosity as just another face of his frustrating and sterile perfection? He has given way, but only to confirm that his saintliness is so saintly that it can even move with the times. Apparent progress serves as a blind to obscure the real problem.

And I would say the same of a parascientist who "understands" human instincts and takes care not to over-react to lapses into deception. By extending scrupulousness, a feeling of progress is achieved. Paradoxically, that feeling of progress is the most unscrupulous cheat of all. We can only begin to face that paradox at a distance, when we remember that more evil has been committed in the name of Christ than ever was in the name of Satan. Paradox is another manifestation of the black hole that deflects thought.

I needed to remind you of that danger before continuing, as the next part of this essay is most important.

What was the anomaly in The Confessions of a Medium? This book confirms the sceptic's claim that most psychics are unscrupulous con-artists; it gives an actual account of the tricks used, and was written by someone who made a living out of their use. Read these accounts and you will never again be impressed by a clairvoyant. Reading these books must be as reassuring to the anti-Geller brigade as witchcraft confessions were to the Inquisition. So much so, that few people seem to notice the anomaly, which is that the writers of these books so often themselves believed in clairvoyance! I find that wierd.

You see we are not dealing with simple-minded souls who are so dazzled by their own spiritual beliefs that they cannot recognise what they are doing; the writers of these books are involved in a more or less cynical exercise in manipulating public gullibility in order to make money. They know all about the subtle, even subliminal, ways of reading another person, and yet they still manage to believe in genuine psychic experience. One writer, having lead the reader through all the techniques, and having described how to practice them until proficiency is gained, says that the process becomes almost unconscious with practice: you look at your clients and immediately just *know* things about them. Yet at times you will find information springing to mind that could not possibly be deduced from outward signs - you experience flashes of genuine psychic ability.

The last chapter in the Doc Shiels book I mentioned, was a chapter on genuine ESP. It was devoted to simple drawing-room experiments in telepathy, the dowsing pendulum, psychokinesis and so on, but done as straight experiments without any chicanery to fake the results. I was intrigued by the writer's justification for including these in a book of fake psychic effects: he said that the aftermath of a conjuror's mentalism act was a good time for genuine ESP experiments, because he had found in his own experience that it produced good results. A demonstration of fake magic powers seemed to make the spectators more receptive to genuine psychic influences - for Doc Shiels believed in genuine psychism.

It was this last observation that struck me more than any other in this quest, for I would not have anticipated it. Putting myself in a parapsychologist's shoes, I would have said that a demonstration of blatantly fake psychism would have sharpened people's scepticism, and made them *less* open to psychic influence. From an occultist's point of view, surely the conscious intent to deceive is not the best setting for the invocation of one's subtler senses? And yet Doc Shiels says it is; and those fake mediums seem to suggest that the long term practice of fake clairvoyance can lead to the genuine thing.

How would you feel if a friend asked you to give a talk on some semi-occult topic, like astrology or dowsing, to a small group of laymen, and you were then approached by someone who introduced himself as a professional astrologer. This person took you aside and made the following proposition. He would come to your talk as an apparent stranger who was rather hostile to the subject. He would challenge you to prove that astrology was not bunk and he would produce his horoscope and demand an interpretation. You were then to take the chart, study it thoughtfully, then denounce your heckler as a fraud. Holding up the chart you would rattle off a brief character sketch (supplied secretly by our friend) then point out that the character was clearly not that of the man in the audience, who was obviously a Geminian and almost certainly born on a certain day two years earlier when Saturn was in .... And at that prearranged moment the man in the audience would blurt out "but that is absolutely incredible! Not only have you accurately guessed my birth-date, but you have also seen through my test, and perfectly described my wife's character, for it was really her chart!"

How would you react to this proposition? I think that, practical joking aside, most people would be horrified by it. If they were on the sceptical side they would feel that there is too much trickery in this field anyway, and the last thing they want is to pollute a serious discussion of the subject with such a fraud. If on the believing side they would be most unwilling to taint their art in this way. "But it would make your audience so *receptive*" says your tempter, "that could only be constructive in the long run". Get thee behind me Satan!

In fact I find this idea amazingly revolutionary. The whole fabric of the sceptic's technique - do a control test on the famous psychic, catch them cheating once or twice, then publish an expose - falls to bits if we say that Uri Geller *has* to perform a few tricks in order to bring through the influence. For now you have to prove not just that he sometimes cheats, but that he never does anything but cheat!

Let us take the story of Geller's trickery nearly to its limits: let us imagine that just once, as a lonely young man, Uri Geller stared at a spoon and it genuinely curled up before his very eyes. It was only when he found that other people were so amazed and incredulous of his claim that he realised what potential it had for a public sensation. Unfortunately, he never managed to do it again. However he was so determined, that he went ahead and devised ways of faking the effect, and has been doing it ever since.

This version of the story might seem like an almost total vindication of the sceptical position, but of course it is not. As was suggested in SSOTBME, a rational world-view is so brittle that it needs only a single miracle to shatter it. A scientist would almost rather accept that Geller can *always* bend metal, than accept that he did it just once. For science is only happy amidst the repeatable: the fleeting singularity is its worst nightmare.

So here is my biggest bombshell: by actually faking magic, we might discover magic. Not just that we should be less scared of the charlatan, less inclined to flee his presence; but that we should actually take lessons from him.

Are you reeling under the impact? Are you falling back in your seats, gasping and goggle-eyed?

If you are not, might I suggest that it would be worth making a little more effort? Embrace wonderment! One conjuror I met who did actually believe in the psychic, shared something with me that is rare among conjurors: he confessed that when he saw a really brilliant conjuring trick, he preferred not to find out how it is done, but would rather just delight in the magic. Somehow that told me something positive about the nature of magical experience. It isn't easy to explain what or why.

Allow yourselves to be amazed, or you will miss a lot. Some people may be so unconsciously defensive, however, that it is once again to late... they will once more bypass the black hole and be unwittingly deflected without feeling a thing. In case this is true in your case, let me try to explain how it happened, to give you a better chance of escaping from this mechanism on the next time round.

You might not have *predicted* that openly fake psychic effects could be a good preparation for genuine psychic effects, nor that a study of how to cheat people could lead to genuine powers: you might even have been surprised by the revelation. But it only takes a little thought, and you soon realise that it isn't so surprising after all. It is very easy to rationalise. For example: you could argue that the fake medium becomes so used to his act that he does it unconsciously, even off-duty he is picking up clues about people; and occasionally these unconscious fragments can well up and surprise even himself. The victim of his own techniques, he thinks he is becoming genuinely psychic.

In this way, any surprise in this essay can be easily banished. But what are we doing in the process? Faced with the unfamiliar, how are we to respond to it? Either it fits the framework of our thinking - in which case it is no longer unfamiliar - or it does not. If it does not, then we either leave it - this is the miracle that cannot fit our world, with nothing to hang on it slips between the structure and falls into oblivion and is forgotten - or else we try to make a fit. Something has to change: unless we are at a crisis point it is unlikely that our structure will change, so usually it is a question of dismantling then adapting, rebuilding, recreating the unfamiliar until it fits our framework. Now we are comfortable with it... but the miracle has gone.

Rationalisation is always possible, just as anything can be banished with a good enough Sword. The question is this: how often do you consciously choose to banish, and how often is it an automatic reaction, and therefore a deception?

We have found the footprints of the trickster, and we have found them very close to home.

The point I am trying to express always slips out of my reach. I too am deflected by that warping of reality. The real point of highest charge, the black hole of maximum distortion, is where the Good-Bad axis crosses our world. If the Christ-Satan axis is detached from this Good-Bad axis, it becomes a simple choice between two types of deity, one of the spirit and one of the earth; all the excruciating paradoxes that Hugo l'Estrange and Dr Sigismund Galganspiel wrestle with in their discourses, are born of the attempt to say "Evil be thou my Good". If we could now detach the Truth-Illusion axis from the Good-Bad axis I suspect that it would begin to look like the simple choice between Hygiene and Fertility. Until those two words are in turn rationalised, you may catch a glimpse of the vital, active relationship that I am trying to convey: Hygiene versus Fertility. When removed from the Good-Bad axis, the word "versus" sounds more like a game than a life and death battle between emotionally charged opponents.

Two practical points are emerging from this quest. Firstly a negative one: do not be too easily put off by fraud, or you will risk losing what you seek. Secondly a positive one, experiment with deception itself. Be a charlatan!

I will flesh out this unusual second approach with two examples.

One branch of mentalism - definitely at the seamy end - is called in conjuring circles "contact mind reading". An example of this is to ask a person from the audience to hide an object while you are out of the room. When you return you hold the person's hand lightly and ask him to concentrate on the hidden object. You then become aware of very small, unconscious muscular forces in the person's hand; and these will direct you toward the hidden object. It takes courage to stick your neck out by attempting such a sensitive task in front of a group of people, but all authorities agree that once you have taken the plunge you will quickly become proficient at it. You become so proficient that it ceases to be a conscious process: hold his hand and you really feel you are being lead by direct thought power! But some authorities claim that you no longer need to hold his hand, one hand on his shoulder is sufficient, or even a short length of chain, with him holding one end and you the other.

This is beginning to sound like real mind reading. Sure enough, the next phase is marked by those writers who describe feats of telepathy or even precognition when there is no longer any physical contact between performer and assistant. [See Nelson's 'Hellstromism' p 21]. By practicing false mind-reading, the conjuror develops the real thing.

I feel like saying "hands up all those who had a go at dowsing, but gave it up because you found it was so easy to consciously effect the pendulum's motion"! Perhaps you should, instead of giving up, have explored this very ability: practiced "cheating" until you became very good at it; doing it with eyes averted, doing it blindfold, doing ot with a pendulum on the end of a stick or hanging inside a bottle so as to be less easy to control. The end point might have been... the real thing.

As in the case of the contact mind reader, we can rationalise one useful mechanism at work. Faking is more fun than scrupulous experimentation. If your psychic practices are restricted to 15 minutes intense meditation a day, there is less incentive to keep it up than there is for the charlatan who can enjoy his developing skills, be encouraged by the spectators' amazement and requests to "do it again". But, after what was said earlier, I must not encourage such rationalisation.

The second example is less exciting, but it is my own, so I can say more about the actual experience of it.

As a schoolboy I discovered Hodson's lovely book on The Kingdom of the Gods. Enjoying the luscious pictures of tree spirits and landscape gods, I wanted to share the fun, but never managed to see them. Through the sixties I sometimes experimented with various techniques for increasing sensitivity and developing auric vision, but with no notable success. I suppose I was always more or less consciously haunted by the danger of self deception: at what point do you begin to kid yourself, become uncritical? I was fleeing from the charlatan.

Around 1981 I rediscovered the book and, being in a desperate frame of mind, tried again. But, as with someone who has attained zen, a tree remained obstinately a tree, however I squinted at it. Then one day I stood by my favourite hawthorn and thought as follows: "What a pity I cannot see trees' auras. If I could, I wonder what sort of aura this one would have? Hmm. I feel it ought to be a fairly vivid red, from crimson to scarlet, but shot through with a network of gold strands. Yes, that would suit it. Then what about that tree over there? oh no, definitely yellowy green in wispy hanging folds."

What was I doing? I was seeing auras, but not *really* seeing them, only imagining them in the sort of way you might imagine how a bare room of a new house might look when it is furnished, how it would look after being decorated. How odd to think that this sort of pseudo-seeing was just the sort of deception that I had so long steered clear of, in my early attempts to *really* see *real* auras. And yet an interior designer's whole income depends upon these 'unreal' imagined images. Just as the writers of those fake psychic books were people whose livelihood depended upon what they were doing: desperados more akin to Rico the Razor than to Professor Wiesenstein.

My new-found game flourished: every tree has a different aura, yet similar species have similar styles. I have resisted the temptation to try to test this discovery, to try to prove that I am not just responding to visual clues as to the type of tree, because it is a growing and delightful diversion. I no more want to dissect it than I want to dissect a pet kitten. I want to enjoy it. If another person describes the aura differently, it would not bother me, because I find this type of perception is more akin to the perception of character than of outer form: in the sense that two people might begin by describing a third person's personality in totally differing terms; yet when they collaborate they arrive at some sort of common description.

If you can catch the spirit of this approach, you will catch another glimpse of that charlatan. The approach is blatantly unscrupulous and amoral, the very stuff of deception, yet it is also paradoxically down to earth and elementary: you just do it, you don't stop to theorise about *what* you are doing. Just like the trickster whose every action is suspect, but who so clearly knows his way around, and makes a living where others simply panic.

I cannot claim that the gift has any practical use, but it was very refreshing to note how quickly it developed once I had got over the initial hurdle of accepting it on its own terms.

This essay is developing a wave formation: a series of forward steps, between which I rush back to defend the rear. Here goes again. I will describe another of the forces that deflect one's mind in the vicinity of a black hole.

You may have labelled me as an anti-rationalist. Labelling is another technique for handling the unfamiliar. It does not depend upon dismantling and rebuilding the unfamiliar, in the way of rationalisation, nor does it just allow it to slip away, like ignoring. It is more akin to casting a net to catch the unfamiliar, then leaving it hanging in the net on some corner of your structure. Unlike rationalisation, this does not destroy the original object; unlike ignoring it does not let it go free. It hangs suspended in its net and is no part of your structure, and it is left, because it is no longer a threat.

So to label this essay as anti-rationalist, is to once more be deflected from the central mystery. I must cut myself out of this net.

Far from being anti-rationalist, I sometimes feel that I am the one person left on earth who knows the real value of reason, of science, of the academic approach. It is a wonderful Sword of Banishment, yet so many seem to confuse it with a Cup of Plenty!

The essential value of reason, or the scientific approach, is that it stops things happening. This is an utterly vital function in a world where most people would agree that too much is happening too fast. The remedy lies right under our noses, yet we create the problem by asking science to do the one thing it has never been able to do, that is to make things happen. As a result a million charlatans have stepped into science's shoes and we never give them their due.

As was argued in Thundersqueak, it is ludicrous to describe the aeroplane as a wonder of science. The Wright brothers were not scientists, they were bicycle makers. On the day of their historic first flight they invited the American Scientific establishment to attend, and the Establishment quite rightly refused to waste time with cranks who were attempting the blatantly impossible. As a consequence, the plane flew. If only scientists had left Uri Geller alone.

As someone who has worked in the aircraft industry, I can assure you that a plane flies despite science, not because of it. Yet I am not belittling science, merely seeing its true contribution. To be utterly precise, it is magic that makes the plane fly, and what science does is to *stop it from crashing*. Indeed the nearest approach made by strict scientific rigour into the "real" world, is via the safety industry.

As reason is the great destroyer - in order to pull you clear of that dreaded Good-Bad whirlpool I will rephrase that remark - as reason is the excellent and much needed destroyer, we should direct it with the care it deserves.

What a pity that man's hunting instincts are driving impressive and exciting creatures like tigers into oblivion. If only the big-game hunters could redirect their urges into hair-raising safaris across the London skyline, in pursuit of starlings and pigeons. Then we would not only be able to keep our tigers, we could also suffer less bird shit.

And what a pity that the scientist insists on chasing the paranormal to its doom, and the historian cannot redirect the urge to shatter myths. They do it too well. Our very own Ellic Howe has delighted us with his skill in stalking the OTO, to the point where there was only one place of safety left for it - namely non-existence.

Such skills must not be wasted, for there is real work for the sword in this world. Several billion pounds are being spent on a cruise missile deterrent, might not some of that money go towards an undercover operation with the collaboration of the secret service? I suggest taking the psychologists out of the parascience field and dropping them behind the Iron Curtain in order to discover the value of Cruise. How deterred by it does your typical Russian military officer feel? Knowing how emotional Russians can be, I want figures of how many soldiers burst into tears, how many resigned from the army, how many committed suicide when Cruise was announced. There is much to do, for I also want some accurate quantitative index of deterrence: I want to know the exact deterrent-value of every million pounds spent. I want to know which is the greater deterrent to world war three: a multi billion pound satellite warfare program, or a late, wet and rather cold spring in Moscow.

And Ellic, your talents are being wasted on an endangered species. The world is crying out for skills like yours, and a far greater challenge awaits you. Instead of chasing the OTO into oblivion, how about directing your attention towards the communist conspiracy within the Labour Party, or the National Front conspiracy behind the Tories? Or why not go for the Big One, and prove once and for all that the CIA is a myth? And please, can I have my OTO back? it was fun.

I would like to be seen as reason's champion, not its detractor. Am I yet free of that net?

I did warn that, in order to write about the Trickster, it might be necessary to assume his mantle: now the time has come to pack up my box of tricks. That would usually signify that a hasty retreat was in the offing: for when people return to reality at the end of his illusions, an angry reaction is liable to set in. But in this case it is the nature of illusion itself that is being studied, so I'll stick around.

The trick that has been played on you is the old trick of presenting a world in black and white: the white light of Truth, of Good, of Hygiene, against the blackness of Illusion, of Bad, and of Fertility. The subject was far too tricky to be tackled without such a trick. But now we awake from the dream, this essay's wave-form accelerates to a frenzied rippling of light and dark, and all outlines are lost until they re-form in the world's true colours. What might almost have seemed clear at times, now passes through chaos.

This is because the rational approach is not scrupulous after all! And yet the very confusion of the situation is somehow a beacon of hope to the traveller, for it recalls the many-layered hypocrisies of highly religious or politically motivated people. In other words, the fact that the rational approach is going to turn out to be riddled with deceit, will 'ring true'. There is something familiar about the path, and that is reassuring. So where is the rational approach unscrupulous?

James Webb writes on the tricky subject of Hitler's involvement with the occult - an area where there are so many rumours that the historian needs to be extremely careful. Was Greiner telling the truth in his interview with Daim? I quote "In his account of their interview, Daim altered some details to test Greiner, and sent the memorandum for the engineer to sign: Greiner corrected the details Daim had changed". So a trick serves as a test of truth! When I think of the many complex ways an individual might respond to finding himself misquoted, I am amazed at the flimsiness of this test of historical truth.

Yet as soon as the academic approach leaves the ivory laboratory and faces the real world, it almost seems as though deception is its only tool. Non-laboratory psychological experiments nearly always seem to involve people doing something whose apparent purpose is a blind for the real test - eg the complex questionnaire to fill in, when it is only the subject's speed of writing that is being tested. Last week a television film showed a road test at the vehicle research laboratory: the lorry was quivering away on a hydraulic test rig, and the engineer explain that it was experiencing a recording of a stretch of British A-road. He took a different disk from storage, fed it to the microprocessor, and now the lorry was bouncing like mad - for this was a recording of a stretch of desert highway in the middle east. Lorries being tested in their dreams, not on real roads! Our future, in world war three, depends entirely upon weapons that no-one has been able to test under war conditions! The very idea of objectivity is a trick; the researcher imagines he is in a sort of condom that gives infinite sensitivity to what he is studying, yet perfect protection against contaminating the subject.

So that is where our pursuit of the charlatan ends: Illusion has an alias, he calls himself Truth.

Mercury-Hermes, the divine trickster, is the god of thieves

and rogues, but also the god of businessmen and scientists. His first trick was the best: he taught us language.

Many yards of language now stretch out behind me, and I wonder why I did it. But I was looking for a remedy, Mercury is also the god of healers.

To return to my first question: how do you respond when your spiritual quest leads to fraud and illusion? When your hopeful pilgrimage to His Inestimable Holiness Swami Sri Chapati, whose adverts in Prediction spoke of the secrets of the universe, leads you to an east-end cockney whose ashram occupies a seedy flat above an Indian take-away? Do you react in anger and disgust, or do you make the best of a bad job and go back laughing to your friends, to expose the old rogue in much humorous descriptive detail?

I sometimes wonder whether, in my childhood when I felt the first calling to the mysteries of the occult, I might have built a little shrine deep in my soul, lit with many candles. Later sophistication buried that shrine and it was forgotten. But I rather suspect that, each time my dreams turn to dust, another candle is snuffed out in that sanctum; and that my anger or laughter is but a mask to hide the disappointment.

The remedy I sought was this: to hope for a new approach, that in future each time a Great Occult Master turns out to have bad breath and wandering hands, I might find not one less, but one more candle burning in my shrine. Amen.

11 - A STRESS ANALYSIS OF A TWISTED KNICKER - Thinkers on the Occult Path

First published in Arrow 18

At the time this essay seemed like an honest attempt by me to rationalise a difficult emotional shambles that I had fallen into. However it was not well received by those who still sensed a vein of bitterness in it that I had failed to transcend.

I recently attended a seminar by Liz Greene on Jung's psychological types, related to the four elements in astrology. One reason for my interest was to see how Jung's four-fold analysis of human types might relate to the four-fold scheme in SSOTBME - an Essay on Magic. There were obvious similarities, even though one is a description of types of *people* whereas the other is a description of types of *worldview*, but how neatly do the two schemes line up? For example: what drives a person to explore beyond the confines of the accepted scientific worldview, and experiment with, say, the magical approach? Is it that they are such natural 'Feeling' types that they choose an approach that encourages this talent; or are they such fossilized 'Thinkers' that they seek in magic to develop the area where they sense that they are lacking?

I have met both types in the 'occult world', but would love to know if my experience agrees with other peoples'. This article is less a statement of a new theory, than a collection of observations put forward for comment.

WEBB OF NO INTRIGUE

Anyone who is weary of all the excitement of the occult scene, and in need of some really tedious roughage on the subject to balance their diet, is recommended to read James Webb's 'The Occult Establishment'.

Ploughing through this bloated heap of ill-connected information I found my mind - starved of ideas - killing time by trying to analyse the book's awfulness. Imagine a large Kenneth Grant book stripped of its slime and its glamour, and you get some idea of Webb's style of writing. As with Grant, Webb's first book on the occult - The Flight from Reason - was not so bad, presumably because a first book is more likely to have been shaped by the comments of editors, whereas later books do not have to work so hard to be published.

Note that my comments on this book are brazenly subjective, for reasons that will later become clear. You could also say that I am bound to be biassed against a writer whose first book on the occult is titled 'the Flight from Reason' (true, I would have preferred a more balanced title such as 'Occultism - a Valiant

Struggle Against the Fetters of Reason'), but there is more to it than that.

The Flight from Reason was quite a good read, because the subject matter was so interesting that it shone through the bad style. But what was wrong with the style? It is not easy to pin down, because the book was not badly written in the sense of being bad grammer, or clumsy, or ill-constructed; it was just that there was something subtly bogus about it. As a retired schoolmaster, I found myself reminded of essays written in order to gain marks: eg the essay urging political moderation, written by a kid who belongs to the British Movement, but is trying to pass an exam marked by a master known for his Liberal sympathies. The book is a marvelous survey of the most delightful 19th century occult cranks and magi, but is written with such an eye on academic respectability that it overshoots the mark. The result is the sort of tight-arsed academic phrasing that might be expected of a book written in the mid-fifties: the sort of writing that would never dare say 'he saw visions of the Virgin Mary', but would always be forced to say 'he purported to see visions...', the sort of writing that is scared of too-popular phrases, and can only handle them between the tweezers of quotation marks.

When reading the sequel, the Occult Establishment, once again the style was tantalizingly bogus. Once again there was an academic respectibility that was a little too good to be true, typified by such wheezy phrasing as:

''Joseph Greiner is not a witness on whose authority one would care to rely heavily.... with the greatest reservations, let us look at Greiner's story.'' and such in-group arse-licking as:

''Some apology may seem necessary for returning to the Protocols [of the Learned Elders of Zion] after the study by Professor Norman Cohn.'' in which one can almost hear the 'chink' of the High Table port decanter being unstoppered.

I was becoming convinced that Webb was striving to impress, but could not really see why such a competent author would allow this striving to ruin his work. Meanwhile I attended Liz Greene's seminar on the psychological types.

Like most tidy theories, the theory of the four types can be quite difficult to relate to the real world: it seems so neat on paper, but not quite so neat when you apply it to real people (I'll return to this problem later); so the most useful function of such a seminar is that it can help to bridge that gap. How, for example, do you recognise a 'Feeling' type? Is he a fluffy, gushy, anti-intellectual? Probably not.

The problem is that we are not raised under laboratory conditions: other pressures exist. For example, there is a social pressure for males not to show their Feelings, and for females not to show their Thinkings. So a naturally feeling male might attempt to repress his Feeling side and pretend to be a Thinker, just as a thinking female might pretend to be a feeler. This is only one of many confusing factors: but I will isolate it for the purpose of this essay. As Liz Greene explained, a Feeling type is not necessarily one that never makes an intellectual statement, but the intellectual statements they make will tend to appear 'wrong' to thinking types, somehow awkward, exaggerated or illogical. As she said this, I at once thought of the book I was struggling with, and her words seemed to explain my difficulty.

The great value of Webb's books lies in the mass of interesting facts he divulges, but it is very hard at times to see any clear thread of ideas linking them - as if Earth were compensating for lack of Air. Rumour and value-judgements are inextricably mixed up with the facts in a way that makes it hard to draw any clear conclusions. When he tells us to look at Greiner's story with the 'greatest reservations', then I am left in confusion, for my greatest reservation is not to look at it at all. When he speaks of occultists who inhabit a universe which "obeys a logic that is unlike that of the rationalist universe of mutually agreed discourse and cannot be understood as logical in its terms" I am sure that the word 'logic' means something different to him, something less precise but more value-laden.

So I felt confident that Webb was a Feeling type. My mistake had been to assume unconsciously that an apparently dry, sceptical book on the occult must be the work of a Thinker. Once I stopped judging it by the quality of its argument, the book was much easier to read. I also remembered being caught the same way before: when I expected the editor of a Rationalist Association magazine to be rational! In fact he was the least coherent arguer I have ever met. He certainly gave the impression of being a man of very strong and clear feelings who had been brought up to believe that only the Thinking principle was manly and true. Unfortunately he seemed to have so little understanding of this principle, that a blind advocacy of the rationalist creed had to play the substitute role. Another example is Patrick Moore: someone with the superficial public image of being a learned expert, yet notorious for his embarrassing emotional outbursts on the subject of astrology!

So how many other Feeling types are there in the crankier extremes of the rationalist establishment? And does symmetry suggest that we should expect to find Thinkers in the occult fold?

It is understandable how social pressures could drive a Feeler, especially a male Feeler, to try to 'prove himself' in a Thinking world. And, because a Feeler is less 'differentiated' at the Thinking end, this is liable to produce a grotesque parody of rationalism (as in the second example) or at least a slightly quirky academic style (as in the case of James Webb). But why should a Thinker become interested in the occult? There is less social stigma attached to being a Thinker (though an extreme Thinker who was a woman might be unconsciously pressurised into acting a more Feeling role), so it is more likely that a Thinker would be not so much pressurised into an interest in the occult, as drawn into it by some inner urge to balance himself. This is perhaps a more healthy incentive than the outward pressure to conform, so we would not necessarily expect to find occult Thinkers taking such wierd forms or standing out so obviously as the Feeling 'rationalists'. So what do we look for?

THE FOUR TYPES

This essay is based upon *my* understanding of Jung's four psychological types: unless the reader shares my vision, it could lead to misunderstanding. So I will digress to explain how I see this distinction. Different circumstances demand different maps. Although the conscious mind can sometimes be pictured as the upper floor of a two storey house, this image can be misleading when it comes to exploring the boundaries between conscious and unconscious. It can be better to see the unconscious as a jungle, in which there is a clearing containing a human settlement - which symbolises a conscious mind.

Each settlement has its own character. For example, different settlements have mastered different skills. One settlement may have distinguished itself by its mastery of agriculture, another by its domestication of animals for food. Another may be especially distinguished by its craftsmanship, another by its sophisticated social structure. Note that all these examples amount to a domestication of some wild element from the jungle: something has been brought into the clearing and tamed for the good of the settlement.

Note also that, just because a certain community is very well developed in one capacity, it does not mean it can forget the other elements. As you stand in the sun-kissed cornfields of an agricultural community it is tempting to think that they have no problems from unruly animals; but that community may well live in terror of the marauding jungle creatures that raid by night.

The analogy with the four types is based upon the fact that different people have to a greater or lesser degree 'tamed' the four elements of Thinking, Feeling, Intuition, and Sensation. Although some 'clearings' are larger than others (ie it is perhaps possible to have a greater or lesser extent of consciousness) it is extremely unlikely that anyone could naturally have tamed all four equally. Such is the difficulty of the struggle to consciousness, that most people only tame one or two elements; in particular it is most difficult to simultaneously master two opposing qualities (eg Thinking plus Feeling, or Intuition plus Sensation). The idea of this analogy is to offset a too-simple picture of there being 'just four sorts of people'. On first acquaintance with the theory of four types, it is tempting to assume that the Thinkers are all lawyers and academics, the Feelers are all social workers, the Sensation types are all technicians and craftsmen, and the Intuitives are all artists. If we were all reared under laboratory conditions, it might turn out that way; but in fact things are much less stereotyped.

For a start, the analogy helps to remind you that a Thinker is not necessarily a person who is devoid of Feeling. As in the case of the crop-growing community described, it is easy to marvel at the cool logic of a Thinker and imagine that such a person has transcended all emotional problems - but the wild beasts of the jungle can still cause pandemonium. Although he may not even know what you mean by the word 'feeling', the Thinker can be utterly at the mercy of the elements that lie outside the conscious 'clearing'.

Similarly, the Sensation type is not totally lacking in ideals, it is just that this element is liable to swoop down in the form of an angelic visitation or an obsessive idealogical conversion. The Intuitive artist may well spend more time agonising about his poverty than creating great art, and the Feeling type can make a fool of himself by being hooked on rationalist 'arguments'. There might be less difficulty if all four elements were equally prized by society; instead, as suggested earlier, there are strong pressures for the Feelers and Intuitives to try to 'prove themselves' in their opposing elements.

If we cannot fall back on such simple formulae as 'if he's a lawyer, he must be a Thinker', how then can we identify the types?

Because the 'tamed' elements run so smoothly, it is easy to overlook them at first; it is the wild, untamed elements that tend to be most obvious to a third party. As in the case of James Webb: it was not his sound value judgements that first struck me, but rather his appalling 'logical' justification of them. This is what is so awful about such rationalists: they denounce some occultist as a fraud, but do it so stupidly that 'sensible' Thinking occultists react by leaping to their colleague's defence; but this reaction is the Thinker's undoing, for very often the occultist does turn out to be a fraud - it was not the value-judgement that was at fault, but merely the grotesque attempt to support it with 'reason'! Patrick Moore makes an ass of himself when he argues that astrology is bunk because 'the sun cannot ever be ''in'' Aquarius because Aquarius is a cluster of stars way beyond the solar system' (as if astronomers never spoke of the sun being 'in' the sky!). However he is quite right to oppose the naive acceptance of a subject that appears to reduce human complexity to a 'mechanical' addition of simple ingredients. I would also be angry if I heard a hard-line Freudian sneering at Jung for thinking that everyone was either a 'lawyer, a social worker, an artist, or a technician' when I know he said nothing of the sort. But, if I could control my wrath, I would do well to admit that no theory should be held blameless for the misinterpretations that it might engender.

It is worth digressing to ask why anyone should want to fall back on such simple formulae as 'if he's a lawyer he must be a Thinker'. Such formulae are a substitute for thought itself. Any scheme that analyses phenomena into a four-fold cruciform 'map' is almost certainly a Thinker's scheme (I suspect that Feelers analyse in threes, if at all, but won't persue that thought). Such schemes tend to be abused by non-Thinkers who look for formulae to do their Thinking for them.

After Liz Greene's excellent discussion of the practical ramifications of Jung's theory of types, I felt that I understood much better. But one or two people said 'oh dear, I am more confused than ever'. My guess is that they were people with undifferentiated Thinking. To give a simple analogy: if you told such a person for the first time about the compass points, they would tend to interpret the directions as a simple formula - eg 'North is where its cold, South is hot, West is where they speak English with a drawl, East is where they speak funny languages'. If you then say that you would build a house on the North side of a valley because it is warmer (facing South), they would respond with 'but now you are muddling me'! Both Thinkers and non-Thinkers agree that Truth must be simple, however the true Thinker is more likely to understand that the practical manifestations of Truth can at the same time be far from simple.

How, then, are we to recognise the Thinkers in the occult world? According to the above description, we should expect them to stand out more for their chaotic Feeling natures than for their logical arguments. Having myself come across plenty of such unruly Feelings, I am inclined to believe that there is a healthy proportion of Thinkers in the occult world!

THE TINKER'S CUSS

I started this article by explaining that I was not trying to lay down any new theory, but rather was putting forward mine own observations for comment. This applies particularly to this section. As will become clear, the first example of an occult thinker betrayed by his 'undifferentiated' Feeling nature... is myself.

For several reasons this makes all my further observations suspect. Firstly, am I merely projecting? seeing in others' everyday emotional problems a phantom that is really mine own? Secondly, as birds of a feather flock together, has my experience of the occult world been restricted to those most like myself? making my observations true but untypical? Thirdly, am I really writing this article (I'll explain that later)?

In view of such doubts let us proceed ''with the greatest reservations'' as Webb would say! I have been aware of two modes of undifferentiated Feeling, and a third mode which I take to be a state of partial recovery. When speaking intimately to some people, you find yourself treading very cautiously. It is as if you are in a jungle and aware of a great python of untamed Feeling lurking in the treetops and ready to swoop down and crush you if you make one false move. With such people your mind races ahead of conversation, trying to avoid the emotive topics, picking words carefully lest the dreaded Feeling-serpent be aroused from its fitful slumber.

Other people can be quite the opposite: in intimate conversation they are models of controlled reserve. Instead of a jungle, you find yourself on smooth paving slabs in a well-ordered courtyard. You admire this triumph of discipline, but find yourself wincing from occaisional jabs of pain. It is difficult to locate the source of these agonies, and you begin to suspect that you have some chronic ailment, and feel increasingly guilty about entering this perfect sanctuary in such a diseased state. The truth is that those jabs of pain come from tiny asps which lurk in the cracks between the paving slabs.

A third type is much rarer: it is the person who has analysed themselves to the point where their Feeling nature is like a romping dragon in a corrale, saying 'ride me if you dare'. The crushing python, the poisonous asp, and the romping dragon are, I guess, one and the same beast, namely undifferentiated Feeling. But the last form seems a partially domesticated and therefore 'better' form to me - even though it seems to evoke disgust from people in the other two modes. As this third is less of a problem, I will concentrate on the first two modes in this essay.

I use the word 'mode' instead of 'type'. So extremely 'opposite' are these two modes that it is tempting to see them as two different types of people. What is worse, it is easy to be fooled by the superficial appearance and think that the first mode is a 'Feeling Type' as opposed to the second mode that is a

'Thinking Type', whereas I reckon that *both* modes stem from undifferentiated Feeling.

The danger of not recognising the symptoms is that these modes are infectious. They do not spread like a virus, so much as like static electricity - in the sense that each mode tends to induce the opposite mode in those who come close to it. In an intimate relationship, the 'electrostatic potential' can mount to such a level that all other activity or communication is overwhelmed.

Having lived through both modes on several occaisions, I think I am well qualified to describe the process from both viewpoints. To shorten the account, I will label the 'wild' mode as the Waterfall mode, and the 'reserved' mode as the Glacier mode. As was suggested above, contact with the Waterfall tends to make you tread very carefully: in other words, it tends to freeze you into a Glacier. You do not feel very good about this, but you can hardly blame yourself, because you see other people reacting in the same way.

This is awful to the Waterfall: the very fact that nearly everyone tends to freeze on them, makes each new freeze the more painful. There is a tendency to remember people you met in your pre- (or lesser) Waterfall days, people who did not freeze so fast, and idealise their memory; for they seem so much more substantial and 'real' compared with those 'superficial', 'repressed', or 'over-polite' Glaciers that now surround you. Depending how much of a Thinker you are, you are more or less inclined to try to explain to these Glaciers how it is their upbringing, or society's conventions that make them so repressed, rather than face the fact that contact with a Waterfall is the biggest repression of all. Yet, as with all such illusions, it has a considerable vein of truth, and this does not make a Glacier in a close personal relationship with a Waterfall feel any better.

So why does the Glacier not become a second Waterfall in these circumstances? The Waterfall tells him that he is 'repressed', that he is only half alive because his feelings are not flowing, that he cannot offer any *real* human communication because of this. The Glacier knows this is true, or is fast becoming true. So why does he not just 'unfreeze'?

I think the reason is because all the Waterfall's talk about *'real'* communication is largely cosmic bullshit. Assuming that it is undifferentiated Feeling that is in fact speaking, and bearing in mind that such 'wild' unconscious processes are not known for their keenness to unite humans in meaningful discourse, then we see that both the Waterfall and the Glacier are basically doing the same thing: they are keeping other humans at a distance. Aiming a fire-hose of Feeling at someone is every bit as effective at keeping them at bay as is surrounding yourself with ice; and to kid yourself that such a fire-hose is a genuine 'communication' is absolute rubbish. I have been faced with a Waterfall screaming 'why can't you accept me as I really am?', when nothing would have reassured me more than a glimpse of the real person I knew that was hidden behind all the foaming torrent of emotion. So what of the other side of the story?

If some personal problem has made you a bit emotional, then a Glacier can seem a thing of wonder. While you swing from rage to depression, here is someone who remains an oasis of calm common-sense. So you cleave to them.

But, just as the extreme Waterfall has developed a neurotic reaction to the inevitable fact that most other people either automatically flee from their presence or freeze over, so also has the extreme Glacier developed a nervous response to the endless flood of Waterfalls that cleave to their cool calm: the Glacier freezes on the Waterfall. The Glacier has no wish to offend, in fact the Glacier knows that, from his apparently superior position, he ought to be able to help the Waterfall who obviously has problems (this is a typical start, but there are variations). So the Glacier is polite and helpful, but treads carefully in order not to hurt the Waterfall's feelings. As a Waterfall has only one kind of feeling, and that is a hurt feeling, this means the Glacier must withold *all* feeling: this is the freezing process.

Unfortunately, even a Glacier has feelings. So the need to repress them in the presence of a Waterfall is hard on the Glacier, and those feelings tend to express themselves unconsciously; those are the tiny asps that lurk and sting the other person.

For a start, the Waterfall often approaches the Glacier from an inferior position; so every escalation of the Glacier's reserve helps to emphasise that very inferiority: the more carefully the

Glacier handles the Waterfall, the more of a cripple the Waterfall feels, the more the Glacier flees the Waterfall's suffocating presence, the more undesirable the Waterfall feels. A Glacier is an expert at 'damning with faint praise'; not through malice, but as an automatic result of blocked Feeling: all praise is faint unless it is supported by a drop of Feeling.

The Glacier's initially superior position can also mean that the Glacier is superficially less hung-up at the social level: while the Waterfall is agonising about whether he dare inflict his tedious presence upon the magnificent Glacier *twice* in one week, the Glacier will drop a casual invitation to 'drop round anytime'. But there is an ambiguous message here: while, on the one hand, the Waterfall wonders if the invitation to come 'anytime' means that the Glacier perhaps really likes the Waterfall, the Glacier, on the other hand, thinks that he must keep the invitation as easy-going and open as possible, in order not to give the Waterfall too strong an impression that his presence is actually *wanted!*

These 'double messages' can be very subtle: the last time I struggled to comprehend why a Glacier's kind smiles evoked such tumultuous feelings in me, I suddenly realised that even in a dim light they were delivered with contracted pupils - normally an unconscious sign of hostility or caution.

The Glacier is always fair and reasonable; the Waterfall admires this, but if the Waterfall has a jealous nature the Glacier will start to be fair and reasonable about the Waterfall's rivals, when the Waterfall would much rather hear some bitchy gossip about them!

At an unconscious level there is now only one topic of conversation: Waterfall: "Look, am I really as awfull as I feel?"

Glacier: "Er... nice weather we're having..."

So the battle rages: the Waterfall putting ever greater pressure on the Glacier in the hope that the ice will finally shatter, and the Glacier ever goading the Waterfall to pour out those feelings which have now grown so bitter that the Glacier would never dare to express them himself. The effort of restraining a Glacier's mounting feelings is exhausting: both parties grow tired in a close relationship, but the Glacier especially so. Perhaps the non-expression of feeling by day means that the Glacier is more dependent on his dreams? Certainly sleep does become an issue, as the Glacier wants to go earlier and earlier to bed while the Waterfall seems maliciously to choose this very time to demand a 'meaningful' confrontation. These battles may have some part in the Cosmic Plan, but they are most destructive on the purely personal level.

I have described some of the negative pressures that drive people into these roles, but there are also positive enticements. Pure evil has never gained much hold on mankind, it always needs an element of good to bait the trap.

Although the 'wrong' committed by a Glacier is subtle and hard to define, the rewards are comparatively straightforward. When you emerge from a hellish session with a Waterfall, it is a relief to unburden your troubles on others - for a Glacier is usually good at explaining another person's awful behaviour. You find that everyone is very sympathetic, quick to condemn the Waterfall and to congratulate you for being so patient with such a monster. This is very encouraging to a Glacier who, minutes earlier, was wondering if he was going round the bend. But when you have heard it all for the zillionth time, and your emotional life is still a shambles, society's adulation grows less satisfying. You will run from adviser to adviser, in the hope of finding one person who can tell you what *you* are doing wrong.

Although the Waterfall's atrocities are much more obvious and easy to describe, the rewards for being such a 'monster' are very subtle and insidious. It is a form of drug addiction. Your torments and your sacrafices have a sort of larger-than-life, intoxicating sweetness that cannot be conveyed in words, but is best compared to certain passages of music, like the passages in Wagner's 'Tristan and Isolde' that mount up and up in yearning spirals without offering any release.

This is so insidious that it is first noticed only as a withdrawal symptom. The Waterfall does have occaisional moments of calm, unmolested by surges of feeling. But these moments do not come so much as a haven of peace, as an icy desert. When the thundering music of your emotions is withdrawn, life is suddenly dry, dead and soulless. Minutes earlier you were an actor on a cosmic stage of superhuman feeling, and now the cold reality of your existence reveals that you are dreadfully ordinary. Whereas the Glacier is reassured to find that he is not alone in his troubles, the Waterfall would like to be the one and only lover in the world.

Once a woman who was suckling a babe described to me the agreeable sensation as a sort of golden glow in the solar plexus. When a Waterfall sits alone and seethes at the thought of the wonderful time his Glacier is now enjoying in the glittering company of all those other magnificent Glaciers, his misery is laced with that golden glow. I am reminded of the mediaeval idea of the witch that suckles demons: those bitter thoughts are the demons that a Waterfall suckles, and in return for sustenance there is the glow of being significant on some cosmic stage: even if you feel insignificant, you are somehow *immensely* insignificant.

As an aside, I should point out to those Waterfalls that, when a Glacier storms out unable to stand their torrents a minute longer, he does not go away 'to have a ball'. Even if the Glacier is at an all-night party, he is probably standing alone against the wall, peacefully wondering why it is that he can only really love the Waterfall in her absence!

I have described some of these symptoms at great length, because I am curious to know if they are as common as I suspect. Some of my friends have similar experiences - but is this just the reason they are my friends?

Meanwhile, while writing this essay, my attention was drawn to two books describing similar symptoms.

WE'RE NOT ALONE!

In Rosenblum's 'Astrologer's Guide to Counselling', in the chapter on 'The Troubled Love Relationship' there is the following passage:

"One of the most common conflicts I have observed... is the following: one of the partners feels that the other is neglecting the expression of care, sensitivity, or emotionality. The other person feels that the partner is exaggerating or making excessive demands and withdraws even further. This turns into a battle of "the demander" versus "the withholder". Both are convinced of the correctness of their position, and the assertions of each only reinforce the fears and conflicts of the other. Although both feel securely ''rational'' in their position, the emotional fact is that ''the demander'' is usually overreacting because of some childhood wound or unmet need, while ''the withholder'' is unconsciously provoking the partner because of fears of intimacy and being controlled..'

For 'demander' read 'waterfall' and for 'withholder' read 'glacier', and it sounds like a generalised account of what I have described.

At the other end of the scale, more particular than general, is Liz Greene's description (in her 'Chart Comparison' lecture in the 'Jupiter/Saturn Lectures') of the two archetypal figures that she names 'the Gorgon' and 'the Iceman'. The passage is too long to quote, so I'll pick out some relevant ideas from it.

The Gorgon is the 'shadow' or extreme, unacceptable limit of the feminine principle, and the Iceman is the equivalent for the masculine principle.

The Gorgon 'is an image of outraged, violated nature. I think it is very difficult for a woman to actually recognise when the Gorgon appears, because one simply falls into her, becomes her. Men spot it instantly.... Her surface complaint may be typical ''How could you have hurt me?'' or, ''If you really loved me you wouldn't have done that.'' Underneath is a deep, ancient bitterness. It is the bitterness of women feeling used, humiliated, trodden upon... It is the thing so many men fear in women, and it is the thing women do not wish to recognise about themselves'. Liz Greene associates the Gorgon with the planet Pluto in astrology.

The Iceman is a 'psychopathic' figure who has no feelings, cannot be touched emotionally. He gives the Gorgon's outrage no value. 'He says icy things like ''I don't wish to discuss this any further''. He tells the Gorgon that she is being irrational and overemotional, and makes clear his revulsion toward her. He says, ''When you've quieted down and can behave like a civilised human being, then we'll discuss it.'' But usually he won't discuss it at all...'. Liz Greene associates the Iceman with Uranus.

Liz Greene claims that she has yet to see a relationship of any importance where these figures do not surface in some form. 'The dynamic between these two is terrifying, not least because these two figures can emerge in two people who actually love each other and don't want to feel like that... It's like possession... Although they are not personal they feed on personal grievances... they can destroy any relationship, no matter how astrologically well matched...'

I recognise much of the Waterfall and Glacier in this, and realise that the most extreme, or likely situation is when the Waterfall is the woman, and the Glacier is the man. But know also this need not be - even in a relationship as described by Liz Greene, a close observer will notice moments of sudden reversal, when the man breaks down or loses control, and the woman immediately turns to ice. This is to me a sure sign that the two modes are a 'tuning in to' or 'possession by' some cosmic polarity, rather than any personal business of the two people concerned.

Sure enough, when the audience asked Liz Greene if the sexual roles could be reversed, she replied that they can. The Iceman can take over a woman's animus. 'He's actually cutting the woman herself down, at the same time as he's saying cold things to the partner... He punishes the woman's femininity and cripples her feeling. Usually he's projected on a man, but you can catch him inside, criticising and cutting down... It says "I don't believe in possessiveness, relationships ought to be free from emotional scenes and demands... I find emotion weak and disgusting". That's the voice. Unfortunately it doesn't sit very well in the feminine psyche. There's an incredible touchiness about it. a real defensiveness... it often takes months and months and months before that woman will actually acknowledge that she hurts, or feels fear, or is lonely or vulnerable.' By way of comparison, (said he, gazing detachedly into the far distance) I must confess that the times that I have harboured the Gorgon have been times when my customary, disarming butchness and objectivity have been somewhat wanting.

It is also true that, although I have been both Glacier and Waterfall, the two modes have not hit me equally. The Glacier mode does seem to have deeper roots. I could hardly describe my experience of the Waterfall mode as 'controllable', but in later years I have been more aware that when it happens it is 'not me'. Instead of becoming a full-blooded Gorgon, I become a sort of battle-ground where an innate Iceman attempts to control an erupting Gorgon. This inner battle probably gives me a curious outer manner, as I blow hot and cold; but this is only conjecture, for I suffer too much inner turmoil to be able to judge how I look! Such behaviour is probably most disconcerting to a female Iceman, who harbours a similar battle but with the roles reversed. As usual in such matters, two people best equipped to be mutually helpful end up being mutually destructive, or at least baffling.

I am inclined to see the Gorgon and the Iceman as the most specific forms of the Waterfall and the Glacier, just as the Demander and the Withholder are the most general forms.

An interesting portrayal of an Iceman figure is given in Dion Fortune's novel 'the Demon Lover'. (The contracting pupils of the cold Justin seemed a bit far-fetched until I recalled my experience of a Glacier who smiled with contracted pupils!) But in this novel, written before the discovery of Pluto, there was no Gorgon response. This raises the intriguing question to the astrologically-minded: has the Iceman become a more-or-less accepted part of our civilisation already, whereas the Gorgon is a comparative newcomer to our awareness (and therefore even more ancient, if you see what I'm getting at)? This might explain why it was easier to describe what the Waterfall did 'wrong', whereas the Glacier's wrongs seemed more subtle and harder to define. We are already living in a partially glaciated world - to the Gorgon's even greater *disgust.* I hate to admit it - but perhaps women really do have the bigger burden!

Typical Iceman stuff this: out there is a world of suffering, and here am I making polite jokes and discussing the 'intriguing questions' raised. As I hinted earlier, who is writing this article? me, or the Iceman who wishes to freeze my last Gorgon invasion?

SO WHAT?

The fact that these two books describe the sort of behaviour I have noted, and describe it as being commonplace, serves to reinforce my observation. But it does not really answer the other questions: is this more likely to happen to Thinking types than to Feeling types? and does it especially often happen to those interested in the occult?

The Gorgon and the Iceman, as described by Liz Greene, are such powerful figures that I doubt that anyone could resist them in a really close relationship; but I cannot believe that a Feeling type would be as vulnerable to such 'possession' as the Thinker - who is more inclined to tie his defences in knots as he tries to explain away what is happening. Both authors make the problem sound utterly universal; but both are astrological councillers, and perhaps people who would consult such councillers are more likely to be open to an interest in the occult?

So the possibility that the rationalist establishment is rich with Feeling types trying to play butch, and the occult establishment is rich with Thinking types trying to balance themselves, remains intriguingly open. But does it matter?

To return to my first three examples: James Webb committed suicide, the Rationalist press man went round the bend, and I am sure that Patrick Moore loses another marble each time an interviewer confuses the disciplines and calls him an 'astrologer'. This does suggest that there is an element of strain in trying to be what one is not. Insofar as the occult path is a path of self-discovery, any information that helps to clarify what it is that you are seeking on that path can be of value.

The Gorgon and the Iceman appear to be denizens of a world that receives more recognition amongst occultists than among the general populace, so if there is any chance of redeeming these figures, then we had better seek to do so in our own lives - before the battles they fight within us erupt into the greater population.

The Uranian Iceman aligns well with the image of the soulless researcher who tackles nature as a box of inanimate puzzles, the scientific establishment that places truth above conscience. That establishment does not control the weapons it creates, instead they are in the hands of political groupings that grow daily more like Plutonian Gorgons in the way they behave. The danger is that these two principles may eventually go into battle with their very own elements - Uranium and Plutonium.

Rather than end on such a political note, I would like to dedicate this essay with affection to all those Waterfalls that have nearly drowned me, all those Glaciers that have frozen me out, and any other perplexed people who have wondered what the hell is going on inside my head!

12 - SIR GARETH AND THE BEAST

First published in Arrow 19

This had its origins in a group magical working of the Celtic current, where we received ''at random'' the name of a Knight and of a Quest and were asked to form a ritual that expressed the two in combination. I received ''Sir Gareth'' and ''The Dragon'', so I read up Sir Gareth and went to Dragon Hill at Uffington for inspiration. There, beneath blue skies on the patch of earth where nothing grows, I conceived the idea for this mystery play on the story of Sir Gareth.

A ritual dramatisation of the history of Sir Gareth of Orkney, conceived and enacted on Dragon Hill, Uffington.

NARRATOR: Step back in time to a younger land where people were few and Nature not man ruled the landscape. Across the open moorland we see a lady in black and scarlet on a fine black horse, pacing with the steady gait that tells of many miles to travel. Her long red hair is held with a jewelled headband, and her head is held high in scorn.

Four paces behind is a young man on a piebald horse; a fine enough horse, but somehow ill-fitting its young rider who seems too ungainly on its back. So also with the young man's attire: it is of noble quality, yet his broad shoulders have outgrown it. His shield and helm are of good workmanship, but do not belong together. From time to time he reaches nervously to touch his sword as if surprised by its presence at his side. He speaks imploringly to the lady's scornful back, in a high, anxious tone that belies his size and strength.

We move closer to this scene, and we merge with the lady. The young man is now therefore talking to us.

G: My name is ...

No, I would rather not tell my name. I'm sorry, it must seem rather silly of me; the least I can do is try to explain why. I suppose it's a question of evading preconceptions.

I was born of a noble family, and brought up as a gentleman. A gentleman's education is a harsh process, geared to breaking wild young souls into an ideal that few can ever match.

One of Nature's stranger tricks is occasionally to bear an old soul in a young body. Harsh lessons, well aimed to mould the wilful passions of youth, merely served to bind my old soul and drive it in upon itself.

I knew that I longed to be a knight. What I did not know was whether this was my soul's true will, or just an imprint of my upbringing.

As I came to Camelot, I envied the blind confidence of my friends, that they could step into this wonderland and straightway demand arms. I had no such certainty. I was even fearful of their expectations and refused to give my name or family. Instead of arms I begged for time; to be tolerated for a year while I tried to get myself together.

I was permitted to work in the kitchen under that bastard Kay...

LINET: It fares thee ill to speak thus of a worthy knight, kitchen scrubber.

G: I am sorry, my Lady, you are absolutely right. But I can hardly thank him for his treatment...

LINET: They say he called you 'Handy Pandy'. I think that's rather funny.

ALL: We think that's rather funny!

G *gazes dejectedly at his large hands:* The joke has long grown wearisome. But I suppose he has fed me well enough.

Anyway, when my Lady Linet arrived at court, telling of fair Lady Lioness who needed a champion, I sensed my destiny.

Was I ready? Was I right? One thing I had learned in my year was that sheer thinking never answered such questions. So I swallowed doubt and fear, and asked leave to play the part.

Thus it is, my Lady Linet, that I am accompanying you to Castle Perilous.

Lady Linet?

Lady Linet!

LINET *crossly:* What is it now?

G *sheepishly*: It's just that I hoped that, if I explained myself a bit, you might grant me the favour of looking at me occasionally.

LINET: What are you talking about now?

G: You mean you haven't been listening?

LINET: It's quite enough to put up with the smell of onions, without having to listen to your prattle too. Do shut up, kitchen boy.

ALL: Yes, do shut up, kitchen boy!

NARRATOR: The sky grows dark, the land grows black. Forbidden to share his burden the young man grows fearful.

In this black land they find a black banner on a blackthorn tree, beside it a black shield and spear. A great black horse stands by, tethered to a black stone whereon is seated a black knight. The slow chomping of the horse accompanies the chattering of the young man's teeth.

KNIGHT: Who goes there?
LINET *quietly*: Look, boy, he's not on his horse. So if you make a bolt for it now, you might just get by safely.
G: What sort of coward do you take me for?
KNIGHT: Ah! Fair Lady Linet! So you have a champion for your Lady Lioness?
LINET: No such luck. It's rather embarrassing, actually; this kitchen knave has tagged onto me and I don't seem able to get rid of him. You wouldn't oblige, would you?
(Gareth seethes)
KNIGHT: If he has the courage to stay while I prepare myself! We'll soon see him on his way.
NARRATOR: The young man and the Knight face each other. The Lady steps her horse backwards to a safe distance.

The young man seethes, then attacks the knight like a maniac, overwhelming him and slaying him. The Lady turns her back.
G: I did it! My Lady, did you see that!
LINET: I didn't have to watch such an embarrassing display of bad taste, did I? But I suppose a knave would be expected to take advantage of a knight when his horse stumbles.
G: My Lady! It was a fair clean fight and I proved myself the better!
LINET: Oh that's what you think, kitchen boy!
ALL: Oh that's what you think, kitchen boy!
NARRATOR: Wearily the young man puts on the Black Knight's armour and mounts his black horse. The armour is barely large enough, but the match of arms and mount does the lad better justice. As if aware of this, he now holds his head higher as he gallops to catch up the Lady; only to falter once more at the sight of her scornful averted gaze.

Now the land grows greener, till they approach a green thorn tree, where there waits a green knight. He sees them first, and recognises the black armour of his brother.
KNIGHT: Ho there, Lady Linet! So my brother is now your consort I see!
LINET: No such luck, sir. Your brother lies slain at the hands of this treacherous knave that has pinched his armour and ...
(Gareth seethes)

KNIGHT: Enough said! He shall die for his villainy!
G: Good sir knight, it wasn't at all like that. Just let me explain ... please!
NARRATOR: The young man gazes imploringly at the Green Knight and at the Lady. As the knight charges, the young man is incensed by the Lady's scorn and turns to face his attacher.

A bloody battle ensues, and rages until the young man has the Green Knight at his mercy. Exulting in his power the young man slowly unlaces the knight's helmet to slay him.

KNIGHT: Good sir! You have proven yourself a worthy knight in battle, pray show yourself a gentleman by now granting me mercy!
G: No way. Unless the lady chooses to plead on your behalf?
LINET: What ridiculous presumption for a knave.
ALL: Oh what presumption for a knave!
NARRATOR: The young man feigns a lethal stab and the knight shrieks. The lady, shaken, steps forward crying 'no!'. The young man gets up and with a low bow releases his victim.

The lady now turns her horse angrily and canters ahead. We follow her towards a magnificent white tower all decked out for a great tournament. There a Red Knight sees her approach, and sees the galloping figure in black armour catch her up.

KNIGHT: Is that my brother the Black Knight?
LINET: No, it's just some rubbish kitchen boy from Arthur's court.
KNIGHT: Oh well, perhaps he's care to pop in for a drink?
LINET: You might just be interested to hear that he not only mugged one of your brothers for his armour, but then went to disgrace your other brother.
KNIGHT: That does put a rather different complexion on the matter, I must say. HOIST YOUR ARMS, VARLET!
NARRATOR: Once more the protesting young man found himself locked in bloody combat. The sound of the lady cheering on his opponent brought out the beast in him and soon the Red Knight lay grovelling for mercy. This time the young man looked straight at the lady and raised his visor quizzically.
LINET *crossly:* Oh all right! It doesn't matter all that much anyway!
NARRATOR: Let us, like true gentlemen, avert our gaze from the lady's shame...

LINET: Hisssss
NARRATOR: ..... and pass on to their approach to a land all blue. As before the lady leads scornfully, waxing eloquent on her favourite topic.
LINET: ... and how I came to be lumbered with this stinking kitchen knave is utterly beyond me. Why I ...
G: But ...
LINET: Shut up, oaf, can't I get a word in edgeways?
As I was trying to say ...
NARRATOR: But the strangeness of the blue land casts its spell over them. The lady falls silent and they continue thus. It is the young man who eventually speaks, quietly.
G: My Lady, why do you ever rebuke me? Have I not done all I can to serve you as a true gentle-knight? As the way gets harder, how I long for a word of encouragement; something to tell me that I'm on the right lines.
NARRAROR: For the first time the lady turns to face her follower. Her scorn no way diminished, she speaks.
LINET: Look here, Peeler, I grant you've proved yourself so far, against a bunch of other meatheads, but now I'm warning you. You're into the big time now. This blue bugger now thundering towards us is really smart. It would need more than just big biceps and beginner's luck to lay him low, I promise you. So why don't you just turn back, like a good little kitchen boy, and run like hell before he catches you?
G: My Lady, I've said it a hundred times if I've said it once: I'm sticking to my word, come what may.
LINET *more softly:* What sort of a lad are you? I've been an absolute bitch to you and yet you insist on taking it like some fairytale nobleman. Please turn back.

Look, you're a pain in the arse, but I honestly don't want to see you hurt anymore. And this Blue Knight is really mean.
G: If you know knew how scared I have been. It was only the pain of your harsh words that gave me strength. There were times enough when I was ready to flee, but one more jibe from you seemed to evoke a wildness in me that I never knew existed. I can only thank you for what you have revealed to me.
NARRATOR: The young man hesitates anxiously, but too late.

The Blue Knight is upon him and battling with all his might. The young man regains his courage in the conflict, and once more presses on to victory. This time the lady is quick to grant her mercy for the Blue Knight's life.

Our two companions are now within reach of the Castle Perilous. Indeed, that night word reaches Lady Lioness of their arrival, and she sends a message of encouragement and a fine dinner to fortify them for the coming day.

Now we find the lady and the young man riding side by side, talking in low tones as if not to arouse the choler of this blood red landscape.

LINET: Look, I'm feeling really bad for getting you into this situation. Turn back now, and I'd quite understand.

G: I'd never forgive myself.

LINET: Well, here's one tip: this next Knight may have the strength of seven men at his best, but in fact his strength increases till noon, then begins to fall off in the afternoon - I think it's something to do with his liver - so if you hang around a bit you will have a better chance of catching him at an off moment.

G: No way. I'm going to take him as he comes.

LINET: You don't have to prove anything to me, you know.

G: I still have to prove it to myself.

LINET: I'm beginning to wish I'd been a good girl and stayed at home doing embroidery. Aren't you scared?

G: Look, can't we change the subject? Tell me about Lady Lioness.

LINET: She's really your type. She read Moral Psychology with the Franciscans.

G: Oh, thanks.

LINET: No, really, you'll like her. And she'll like you. I only fear you may get carried away too quickly. I suppose that is why I've tested you so harshly.

Just look at that castle, doesn't it give you the creeps?

G: Madame, I'm going through hell in this hot, red land. I wish the good knight whose armour I'm wearing had known a little about the heat absorption properties of black bodies. I also wish he'd made it easier to get it off, for my bowels are troubled with fear.

LINET *coyly:* So shall I say some more bitchy things to make you angry again?

G: Thanks, but it isn't quite the same now. Tell me more about your sister instead.

Hey, what the hell is that?

LINET: Some forty odd previous contenders, now hanging, rotting in the trees. I told you this knight had no mercy.

G: The bastard, the absolute bloody bastard!

LINET *quickly:* Oh, that's nothing! You should hear what he does to little children...

G: Just wait till I get my hands on that bastard!

KNIGHT: Halt, you two!

So my Lady Linet has found another champion! Another little hopeful to swat and hang in my collection!

G *pointing with his spear at the hanging corpses:* What's the meaning of this, you bastard!

KNIGHT *laughs mockingly:* My, a pocket philosopher! What's the "meaning" eh?

Might I ask your "meaning", knave? What can be the "meaning" of death? Methinks the last part of your question contains the answer to the first part, considered analyti-

G: Shut up, and fight!

NARRATOR: The young man charges like a mad bull, and the Red Knight coolly sidesteps and cuffs him on the shoulder. The young man staggers, then regains his composure.

A mighty battle ensues. All day they fight, at times resting to gather strength, and suck segments of oranges. At such times the young man sobs and shakes with weariness and loss of blood, but the lady points to the castle and says her sister is there at a window, waving encouragement. With that the young man each time rises again and tells the Red Knight to raise his bloodied arms once more. Each time the Knight rises more uncertainly, till at last he falls in battle not to rise again. The young man flops onto him, gasping, and begins to lift his dagger to strike.

KNIGHT: Good sir, you have well proven yourself in battle to be the mightiest in the land. I beg you, good sir, now show equal standing as a gentleman, and let me live!

G: You must be joking, you cruel bastard! Just explain those forty brave knights swinging in the trees, and why you didn't spare their lives, if you can!

KNIGHT *with renewed energy at the joy of having someone to listen to him after all these years:* Well, it's like this you see. That's the last thing I ever really wanted to do, but I once loved a lady, and she absolutely insisted I commit all these atrocities ...
G: Gosh, you poor thing! How beastly! I know just what you mean, Ladies do make us do the most dreadful things, don't they?
LINET: Hissss
NARRATOR: And so the young man and the Red Knight help each other to their feet, shake hands, and swear undying friendship. The young man tidies himself up a bit then rushes eagerly to the castle.

It is locked.

He tries every door, but the doormen say they've had their orders. In despair he shouts to Lady Lioness. A voice replies from behind the door.
LIONESS: Be calm, good sir. Full nobly have you fought for me, but your admission is not timely.

Depart hence, and aspire to the innermost secrets of knighthood. Return in a year's time and I shall be waiting in joy.
G: A year! How could you! I've given the best blood in my body to get here.
LIONESS: Believe me, my champion, I do not say this to taunt you. How could your longing ever exceed mine? I swear that I will think only of you for these twelve months. Please wring my heart no longer, go forth and grow in wisdom.
NARRATOR: Muttering a thousand curses on the ways of womenfolk, and temporarily certain that the whole wide world holds not one drop more of undiscovered wisdom, our hero trudges into the sunset.

So do we have to wait a year to hear the outcome?

Not so. For curiosity overcomes wisdom in Lady Lioness' breast. She hatches a plot to discover her champion's real identity. The outcome of this ruse might have been foreseen: in disguise she meets her champion in a nearby castle and their love is at once confirmed. The young man has never seen Lady Lioness at close quarters, so does not realise who she is.
G *to himself:* Gosh, isn't she terrific! If only this Lioness woman was half as good as her, I'd really have something worth waiting for next year!

NARRATOR: Unable to contain her rapture, Lioness confesses all. The lovers embrace in ecstasy.
G: When?
LIONESS: Tonight!
G: Where?
LIONESS: In this hall!
G: How?
LIONESS: I'll come to you!
G: DARLING!
NARRATOR: Behind the curtain Lady Linet shakes her head and sighs. Only magic can save the situation now. We find her stirring strange potions in a cauldron.
LINET: Why do I always get the unpopular parts?
ALL: Don't worry, Linet, you're one of us!
NARRATOR: That night finds the young man pretending to be asleep in the hall. The sight of Lady Lioness in her ermine mantle ends the pretence. Eagerly they embrace. At the point where Modesty reaches to draw the curtain we stay her hand. For lo! a thousand flames light the hall and a knight is suddenly there calling challenge.

The young man springs to his feet and grabs his arms. The fight is bitter. Our hero is the victor but, maddened in his lust, he hacks off the knight's head and hurls it out of the window, before collapsing wounded on the floor. His recovery is hardly hastened by the sight of Lady Linet sticking the knight back together again.

Ten days pass before the lovers can repeat their secret tryst. This time the young man has his sword at the ready. But it does him no good. The flaming knight fights with superhuman strength and delivers a wound most grievous to a loving man, before falling to the young man's fury.
ALL: Alas, poor youth.
NARRATOR: Alas for those whose ardour bypasses wisdom. It was Lady Linet who, by herself playing the Dragon, evoked the Dragon power in our hero. It was she who saw how he slowly learnt to control the power, to the point where he was match for the wiliest opponent. In his final battle he even learned to raise the power through love as well as hatred.

But did that mean that he was ready for his Lady Lioness? Oh no! For this phantom knight of a thousand flames was just the vision of his own Dragon power, revealed to him through Linet's craft.

And did it serve his love? No, it merely came between him and his lady. She should have trusted her earlier wisdom, and kept him at bay till this lesson had been less painfully learned.

Can we expect him now to understand?

Perhaps the answer awaits some future people: an older Albion heavily populated with older souls: uncertain knights who also beg their rulers for food and games, instead of recognition and adventure. Perhaps they too will only know the Dragon power through its evocation in mob enthusiasm? Perhaps they too will ignore their feminine wisdom?

Or Perhaps they will at last find this mystery's solution, where our young man has failed?

G: No! Let me speak once more!

There's nothing like lying wounded for giving a young man time to reconsider. I see now how Lady Linet was right all along, blast her!

It was that same Dragon that came between Lioness and me, and I set out to kill it. Yet the oldest tales tell not of killing dragons, but of cutting off their heads. No ordinary act of butchery. Some even say it cannot be achieved by men, but only by the merciful assistance of the Archangel Michael. Be that as it may, men have always interpreted the tale in terms of killing the beast. But it alone knows that it cannot be killed: every piece hacked off by raging men merely spawns further Dragons of its kind!

So what is this 'cutting off the Dragon's head'? In the gentlemanly art of breaking in young horses, we were told not to 'give the wild horse its head', lest it should run amok. To love a horse was to know when to be its 'head'.

So was the tale of cutting off the Dragon's head rather more an instruction to deny it total freedom, never to let it run amok? The "middle way" that always sounds so boring - until you actually try to put it into practice.

Armed with this pearl of wisdom I felt ready to get my hands on lovely Lioness once more. But fate had other plans: My Lady was summoned to Camelot.

It appeared that 'Mummy' had turned up at Arthur's Court and spilled the beans about my oh-so-noble background.

Before my Lady left, we made hasty plans for my 'comeback': she was to organise a bumper tournament, and I was to turn up incognito and sweep the field. I guess I still had something to prove!

Anyway, we did it. I was bloody marvelous that day, knocking down knights like skittles, but this time strictly to the Queensbury Rules of a tournament. I never quite knew when I should stop and unmask myself - it always seemed that I needed just one more victory to really show them - but fortunately someone recognised me and blew my secret before I made a real fool of myself!

So there we were, hugs and kisses all round and, of course, the hand of my Lady Lioness in marriage.

I have cut a long story short, for I know you are really more interested in Dragons. And I'm quite sure that you've had enough of the prattling of a kitchen boy.

Even if this particular kitchen boy just happens to be ...

SIR GARETH OF ORKNEY!

13. BLAST YOUR WAY TO MEGABUCK$ WITH MY SECRET SEX-POWER FORMULA

Love that title. Just had to put it in for the sake of giving the book a nice name.

But what shall the essay be about?

Someone said it would suit my style if, having given that title to the collection, no essay of that name were to appear in the book - but I feel that would be a bit naughty. I must make an effort and imagine that I have actually been commissioned by someone to write an article on a particular magical topic.

Trouble is, I don't have a secret sex power formula.

Ok, you don't believe me. You think I'm only saying that to keep the secret secret.

Well, I've never had megabuck$: it's taken me ages to scrape up the cash even to publish this book and I know I'll probably have to sell at a loss to get rid of the thing in the end.

That's why I like the title. It's so ironic.

I really suppose this has to be an article about magical effectiveness. So here goes.

I love the occult literary cliche where the listless and disenchanted young seeker gets into conversation with a mysterious stranger in a seedy secondhand bookshop... and finds that he or she has been "chosen" by a highly secret and exclusive international elite who use occult knowledge to shape world history for the benefit of mankind - in the face of inhuman evil forces, of course. The Rosicrucian dream.

I gave up hopeful hanging around secondhand bookshops years ago. The rule of thumb seems to be this: the more occult knowledge, the less magical power; the more magical power, the more ignorance and bigotry.

In fact, the only way to make megabuck$ in the occult is to take some brain-numbingly simple principle like transcendental meditation and sell it like crazy.

I have actually tried quite hard to make megabuck$ by magic. Don't laugh, but this very book is a last dying ember of a dream that I tried to realise back in 1970. If Thatcherism gets to heaven before me, and wordly success becomes the criterion for admission, then I am doomed to eternal damnation for sure - along with nearly every occultist I know.

Does that sound like the final condemnation of magic? The deathbed revoking of a lifetime wasted in occult studies? Can humanity now forget the magical quest for the delusion and folly that it so patently has been proven to be by this confession coming from a leading occult theorist (well, someone once called me that)?

Let's get this in perspective. I also went through a religious phase as a child, and I didn't find religion very effective either. In fact the same laws seemed to apply: religious awareness seems to be in inverse relationship to worldly effectiveness. And you only make megabuck$ with religion by flogging pap.

I have also tried to make megabuck$ scientifically - and know a number of fellow Cambridge graduates who have put even more effort into such endeavour but with little obvious success.

Funnily enough, my only glimpse of relative wordly success has come through the application of art. Putting on a decent act in interviews, and coming up with a few creative ideas for proposals, have together earned me more modest bucks than all of magic, religion and science put together. But never megabuck$.

So the real conclusion of this experience must be that humanity should finally forget all about religion and science as well as magic... and try a bit harder at art.

Alternatively, humanity should stop drawing sweeping conclusions based on daft criteria.

As usual I am reminded of Jung's classification into psychological types with its division into two polarised pairs: sensation versus intuition; thinking versus feeling.

Development in one of each pair seems to militate against development of its opposite. If a sense of personal power comes from a well-developed feeling nature, then we expect that sense of power to be lacking in a well developed thinking nature. Thus we find that those who have great knowledge can seem rather ineffectual - and it makes no difference whether it is occult, scientific or any other type of knowledge.

Curious, really, in view of the fact that the information industry keeps insisting that "knowledge is power". Perhaps it is - just as much as matter is energy - but that in both cases it takes one hell of a lot of application to transform between the two states. It is as difficult to make a lump of matter reveal its energy as it is for a knowledgeable man to reveal any great power. And when people are wielding power they tend to come across as thick as bricks.

Similarly it is a common observation that the intuitive person is not very good at handling practical affairs - like the cliche of the brilliant artist who cannot make money. And those who are good at making money tend to show very little imagination in using it.

So if I fail to become rich despite the application of magic, religion, science and art, perhaps it is not magic, religion, science and art that have proved ineffective, but rather myself?

And if I fail in love, perhaps it is not magic, religion, science and art that have proved powerless, but rather myself?

In each case the fact that I end up with more knowledge and wisdom, rather than results, says more about me than my methods.

Perhaps there are many thoughtful intuitives drawn to magic because they seek an unconscious balance of their natures, and that the poverty and wordly ineffectiveness of many magicians is a reflection of their nature more than it is a demonstration of magic's ability?

It is particularly in England that we witness this problem. Magicians in some other countries seem to have less difficulty in holding down good jobs, becoming reasonably rich, or achieving some sort of eminence. So perhaps national character plays a role too.

Aries is the traditional astrological ruler of England, and it does reflect in a certain pioneering spirit that likes to start up new ideas or projects but is not very good at carrying them through to the finish. We rather pride ourselves on having good ideas that other nations exploit, and there is a certain self-defeating streak that sees wordly success as somewhat vulgar. That aligns with the creative artist who struggles to make money while deeply despising it.

I suspect that the historic success of the British Empire owed a lot to, say, the greater tenacity of the Scots (ruled by Cancer) although one would expect the Aries nation to take the credit.

This is beginning to look pretty bad. Myself and English occultism are doomed to failure. So what the hell are we all doing?

I know a German magician who really is quite proficient at making money and achieving success, and I have heard him proclaim ''magic is about power''.

Certainly if I think back to earliest childhood hopes about magic there was a yearning to be able to make things happen: to be able to point one's finger and make enemies crumble or thunder rumble, to wave one's wand and turn lead into gold at a stroke. With greater maturity this persisted as a more general desire to be successful, to ''prove'' magic by achieving more than the non-magician... and so on.

But once one got really into studying real books on real magic all that started to look a bit kitsch. One was on the spiritual path now. Instead of doing a spell to make the girl next door fall in love with you, it was considered more comely to transmute one's base desires and become a higher initiate (perhaps then she would love you?).

The question of power seems to be forgotten at this stage of development. In its place there is the idea of transformation, or of perfecting oneself.

Indeed, when you consider the number of occultists for whom

magical practice consists of meditation, seasonal rituals and ''celebrations'' rather than doing spells to make things happen, the idea that ''magic is about power'' might seem far-fetched. Even when an effect is desired, it is likely to be something vague and open ended like ''planetary healing'' instead of ''megabuck$''.

At this level it is tempting to dismiss the idea that magic is about power and making things happen as a childish or uneducated view, whereas ''real'' magicians know better. They've grown out of those naive desires - or so they think.

My experience of the Abramelim operation lead me back through these layers. When I was preparing to do it I was of course not interested in the final chapters which gave the magical squares for doing spells: flying through the air, summoning an army, knowing secrets, finding treasure etc. I could see such spells as pure superstitious nonsense and that the real magic lay in the earlier chapters with the careful work, the purification and the dedication. I was not going to do this with any delusions about becoming a miracle-worker, it was all about becoming a wise magician.

However, six months of solid magical endeavour is a great revealer. After a while I made the embarrassing discovery that part of me still did want to be able to do spells just like the book said. I'd unearthed that child in me. The child that resented growing up because it equated maturity with disillusionment.

It said the reason I didn't want to do spells was because I was afraid they would not work. As long as I directed my magical endeavour into vague things like ''spiritual advancement'', ''wisdom'' or ''improving the world'' then I could go on kidding myself that it was working. But if I tried to blast my way to megabuck$ I would be rapidly disillusioned.

I suspect that quite a lot of today's magicians are doing the same thing: limiting themselves to a form of magic that cannot fail because it has no clear standards of success. So when the German magician said ''magic is about power'' he was not speaking as a naive soul who had not yet learnt about ''real grown up'' magic, instead he was reminding his audience of something that had been swept under the carpet.

This is one of the contributions that Chaos Magic has made

(for he was a chaos magician): it has reacted against the wishy-washy tendency in New Age magic and reminded us that the impulse to make things happen is not childish, but should be respected and restored to its place in magic.

This is healthy because it clears a certain amount of bullshit. If you want the girl next door to fall in love with you it might be better to do a spell than to repress the urge on moral grounds. In the first case either your spell will fail (in which case you have learnt something about your technique) or else it will work (in which case you are almost certainly about to learn something about the longterm folly of all such spells). If, however you deny the impulse "because it is creates bad karma to interfere with another's will", then you are liable to slip into such hypocrisy as I suggested above: going for spiritual perfection because you unconsciously believe it will make you more loveable. It's the old story about going out and being prepared to make mistakes with your eyes wide open - rather than sitting at home playing safe.

So I respect the view that magic is about power, but do not think it represents the whole truth.

Austin Spare said some harsh things about ceremonial magicians in his Book of Pleasure. In fact he went a bit over the top, probably because of his recent contact with the remains of the Golden Dawn crowd. But I did like his observation that *"their practices prove their incapacity, they have no magic to intensify the normal, the joy of a child or healthy person, none to evoke their pleasure or wisdom from themselves"*.

I particularly like "to intensify the normal". Consider the following question: what would be your idea of the perfect party? It is natural to start to think in terms of a fine, warm evening, a big building with lots of garden and a lake, brilliant music with a live band, lots of drink and good food, fascinating people and so on. But think again: it would be quite possible to get all that together and still have a party that failed to swing.

On the other hand, there are times when a few unlikely people get together in an odd place, someone lights a fire, and a few tins of beer are all that is needed to create a magical, memorable evening.

In the first case the impulse is to make a good party by

creating the conditions for it. That is like exerting magical power to make something happen.

In the second case it ''just happens'' that you catch the spirit of a good party, and a dull evening is transformed. That is an example of the other aspect of magic: magic as transformation.

If you accept that the real aim is to make life good, then magic that can transform the dullest moment into pleasure, magic that can ''intensify the normal'', magic that can make even poverty seem like fun... such magic is every bit as valuable as the power magic that would make you rich. So if a group of wierdoes choose to prance about at Stonehenge in order to ''celebrate Gaia'' or whatever, and if they thereby enjoy an experience of Stonehenge that is far more intense and magical than that of the average tourist who goes there, then I would be the last to condemn them for having ''wishy washy'' magical objectives.

Think of the dreariest possible situation - let us say commuting to work in a dull office on a wet winter Monday morning and getting caught in a traffic jam. Note that I am not describing the *worst* possible situation, but simply the dreariest - it is dreary because it is so ordinary and commonplace.

So the first thing to realise is that the situation is not actually that bad in terms of absolute human agony: any Siberian prison camp victim, any person dying in the desert during the Gulf War, or anyone undergoing torture in a South American gaol would give anything to be transported into the peace and comfort of a warm car in a London traffic jam with nothing worse to look forward to than a dull day in a boring office. You could call it Heaven.

So here is one simple example of the power of transformation magic: if you are able to evoke ghastly scenes of horrible alternative situations as you sit in your traffic jam on a wet Monday morning, then you might come to believe that you are in Heaven.

If that sounds a bit too much like hard work, try this example. The same office, the same traffic jam and the same time, but there is one big difference: you have just fallen madly in love with one of your colleagues who works in that office and have been waiting all weekend for the rapture of his or her company. Now your heart is singing in the rain - and you are indeed in Heaven. The dreary situation has been turned to gold by the magic of transformation.

As a child I used to be fascinated by the Surrealist movement. I loved to read about cafe society between the wars, and I used to think what fun it must have been when there was all that revolutionary fervour and intellectual stimulation in the air - ''if only it was like that nowadays''. This was, of course, sheer nostalgia - another powerful agent in the magic of transforming dull reality into gold.

Twice I have spoken on this subject to a group of people, and what I did at this stage was to ask them to close their eyes and listen carefully. I then describe our present situation from the nostalgic viewpoint of, say, thirty years in the future. ''It must have been the early 90s - yes, there was talk of the Gulf War, a sense of urgency and change as old empires collapsed and re-shaped, a feeling of expectancy as the millennium approached... we came together, from many walks of life, we came together in the name of magic to explore new and challenging ideas...'' and so on.

I then point out to them that nothing I have said about our situation is actually false, all I have done is to miss out the commonplace facts as we experience the present moment - such as a sense that the seats are uncomfortable, that the speaker is going on too long and lunch is getting delayed, that the audience is the same old crowd who turned up last year...

''You are looking at the world through rose coloured glasses'' is how a cynic would put it, but then I explain that most people who use that expression fail to understand the *real* effect of rose coloured glass. They imagine that it superimposes a nice colour on the scene, a colour that does not belong there. However, this is optically incorrect: all rose-coloured glass can do is to filter the transmitted light and remove every colour except rose. It simply reveals the rosiness that is there by removing all other colours: that is the scientific actuality. So I argue that rose coloured spectacles do not give a falsely optimistic view of reality, they simply (from a rosy point of view) reveal the truth.

So, when I make my audience close their eyes and I weave a magically entrancing picture of our present situation, I argue that I am not putting a false glamour onto a dull everyday reality. Instead I am revealing the magic that really is ever-present.

Going back to that bored commuter. A very clever photographer could follow him to work and catch just the right shot - the frustration of a bored commuter in today's modern city - and it could become an award-winning cover for a colour magazine. Has the photographer somehow artificially ''glamour-ised'' the scene, or has he rather (as I am suggesting) focussed in on the archetypal essence that really exists in that situation? The latter explanation fits the actual mechanics of the photographic process far better than the former one.

That is to me a vital part of the magic of transformation: it is less often an aggressive act that imposes a new state or experience, more often a question of an alchemical distillation of the quintessence of what actually exists.

So if a bunch of New Age wierdoes talk about ''contacting power'' as they prance about and wave crystals on Glastonbury Tor, then I laugh at them merely for the joy of laughing at archetypes - and I do not automatically assume that they are deluded people who only enjoy what they are doing because they have lost touch with and denied the realities of this brutal existence. The power and magic of Glastonbury Tor is really there - if only because every moment and every place is full of the magic of sheer being - and I salute any process that might lead to rediscovering or revealing such magic.

I have described a sort of evolution.

We begin with magic as a natural (and therefore not unhealthy) desire to exercise power.

Experience teaches us that we need to work first upon ourselves before exercising power, and so the idea of self transformation becomes paramount. This is good in itself, but it can become an excuse for no longer interacting with the world: so much aware now of our own limitations we no longer dare to exercise power even when it is needed - we are afraid to do magic in case it doesn't work.

So a revival of power magic is a welcome and positive step that revives the spirit of magic - unless it encourages us to deny the validity of transformational magic.

The latter then reminds us that there can be limits to power and that it is also important to accept things as they are in order to make the best of what is.

There seem to be two polarities at work here: idealism versus realism and control versus acceptance. Idealism wants to impose better things, either by exercising power to make things happen, or else by nurturing transformation; realism does not have to mean strangling power by wallowing in life's awfulness, it can equally mean looking for what is good in order to nurture its growth. The interaction of the first polarity with the polarity of control/ acceptance leads to these differences of colour.

Idealism and Realism

Looking back over the years, are you aware of times when the air positively crackled with excitement at the feeling that things were changing, the world becoming a better place, that you had at last found your real direction, a purpose for living?

And do those times contrast with periods of emptiness, when dreams are shattered, disillusionment sets in and the world seems not only to have rejected all the hopes you had but, what is worse, seems to have corrupted those very hopes and bred monsters from them?

You see this in society. The 60s dream becoming 70s disillusionment becoming 80s greed. A psychedelic revolution that spawned a load of megastar addicts who either die or turn into anti-drug preachers (why can't they admit that they might have needed the drug experience to become what they now are?). A Marxist revolution that settles down to totalitarianism.

It is so often a ''revolution'' that provides the excitement, yet which breeds monstrous forms in reality - and that provides the clue. For Uranus is the planet of Revolution in astrology.

Uranus is a very ancient god in Greek mythology - way back before Jupiter and all that crowd. Out of Chaos came just two gods: Gaia, Goddess of Earth, and Uranus, God of Sky or Heaven. Two polar extremes drawn by their very oppositeness.

Gaia would seduce Uranus who would descend on Gaia and impregnate Her. Many children were born, but they were monstrous children, grotesque giants. Uranus, having the vision and purity of a Sky God, was appalled by the ugliness of these children. They seemed like a corruption of the divine essence with which he had fertilised Gaia, like a mockery of all He had dreamed of giving Her. So he used to kill these children - all of them.

Gaia loved Uranus and could see that He wanted to give Her something better, but She from Her practical point of view began to realise that She was ending up with nothing at all. It's all very well insisting that none of these children are good enough - but She would rather have a monster than just a dream of perfection.

So She ganged up with Her latest monster child called Chronos and warned Him in advance of His probable fate. Chronos armed Himself with a sharp sickle and, when Uranus came to get Him, cut off Uranus' balls and chucked them into the sea.

Thus emasculated, Uranus fell from power and Chronos became the new King. But you know how it is with abused children: He developed the same habit and took to eating his kids until Jupiter started the next revolution and became the final Sky God...

Meanwhile, back in the sea, the testicular creativity that Uranus had lost expressed itself in a last autonomous act: his balls transformed into the Love Goddess Venus who was then born from the waves...

That is such a brilliant myth, so bulging with cosmic truth. Taking the example of Marxism: a bright new vision descending on earth and impregnating mankind with revolutionary fervour. It gives birth to many little squabbling groups which are strangled by their own idealism. Anyone who has attended revolutionary meetings 'where all is well until actual practical propositions are put into action and then no-one can agree anymore', will know what I mean by that last sentence. But one such child, Bolshevism, has the cunning to castrate its father, to banish the visionaries and usurp the throne of world communism. Although Marxism becomes utterly discredited in the process, something has survived in the form of those cast-off testicles. Maybe it is the gentle, caring vision of Socialism that rises from the waves to seduce the other governments of the world?

If you, gentle reader (ok, I know you are actually a psychopathic hired mass murderer for an international terrorist organisation, probably crazed on amphetamines and blood as you read this, but I guess you have your gentler moments too), only knew the vision that has inspired my writings in this collection of essays. Idea upon idea that came to me like scintillating streaks of lightning dazzling the dark - each one the sort of idea that merited a great book, a great public debate, a new world movement. But look at the result: filtered through my own language ability, dragged onto paper, flogged round publishers and eventually spun into some sort of shape by my poor old Mouse... even as I write these words I am strangling my children! Even in this paragraph I have included an assumption about the reader that will alienate me from tight-arsed academic respectability.

Bless Li Greiner who reviewed Words Made Flesh in Gnosis, and pointed out the self-defeating quality of my own bitterness. I hope my letter to him gave some idea that there is a form of love in Uranus' destruction of His own children - a sadness that I have not done justice to my vision which makes me want to tear up the canvas - and that makes publication an even greater trial. It is a very Aries thing and, as suggested above, a very English thing to do - because it is so clear to any outsider how English inventors manage to ruin their own work at the same time as cursing the world for not taking it up. Bright little companies botching their marketing and splitting up to spawn other bright little companies. The eternal on-going revolution that results in us staying always so much the same. Oh this septic isle.

Anyway, there's a sort of maturity in putting forward my very pain as yet another bright idea. I do feel that the myth of Uranus is very potent because it shows so clearly the love/hate between the ideal and the real, between Fire and Earth, Wand and Disk, or between intuition and sensation - as you will. I feel that it has been a major factor in human affairs and that it would now be the most important factor were it not for the rise of relativity written about in another essay (The Law Is For All) in the next volume in this series.

In that essay I argue that Perfection has had its day. If we take magic as an example: there is a traditional problem of old Aeon magic and it goes like this:-

I want to be rich, happy, sexy, powerful....

Hey! I've discovered this thing called "magic" that can make you rich, happy, sexy, powerful...

Wow! I've been reading about magic and I've discovered that it's really quite simple to become rich, happy, sexy, powerful... as long as you do one thing - you have to become perfect first.

So how do you know when you've made yourself perfect?

Oh shit. You know you are perfect when you no longer WANT to be rich, happy, sexy, powerful...

Now modern magic, as typified by chaos magic, is no longer dominated by notions of perfection. In Pete Carroll's Liber Chaos he does not exhort the aspirant to first perfect themself; instead he provides formulae which relate one's magical effectiveness to a number of factors such as the probability of the outcome happening by chance, the relative strength of the magical link, and one's own ability to achieve gnosis.

So I do not see the clash between perfection and reality being so much the central problem of magic now. In its place I see the clash between ecstacy and deliberation.

Acceptance and Control

In Pete Carroll's equations of magic referred to above, the effective magic factor is proportional to the amount of gnosis - which we can loosely translate as ecstacy for the purpose of this essay - but it is also proportional to the *lack of* conscious awareness.

This is the problem I see in modern magic. To be really effective and powerful you need to be in a highly ecstatic state of gnosis and with very little conscious awareness. In its extreme state that grows very close to lack of all control.

From the point of view of power magic this paradox is a bit disturbing: to exercise real power you need to abandon control of that power. For the magic of transformation it is less worrying because you are not so much aiming to control situations as to open yourself up to accept their true essence - and the flow of power that results is just an expression of that magic. This paradox seems to be as deeply ingrained as the uncertainty principle - a real limitation in manifestation.

Whereas the last section dealt with the polarity of the Wand of Idealism and Will impacting the Disc of Matter and Realism, this section looks at the struggle of the Sword of Analysis and Control versus the Cup of Acceptance and Ecstacy.

As before, I see this as an important problem for humanity, and this one is becoming even more important now - because the rise of information and other technologies is presenting governments with greater opportunities for control than ever before, while the persuit of such control seems to invoke paranoia in government and in the people it invokes ecstatic wildness and drunkenness of the senses.

As without, so within. I was very struck when I read the biography of L Ron Hubbard, founder of Scientology. In the early 50s he presented the world with a simple form of psychotherapy that promised a new age. Recognising that our unconscious minds held enormous power, but that the power was trapped and convoluted like a knotted mass of serpents because of past conditioning, Hubbard proposed simple techniques that would allow individuals to untie those knots and release the full potential of the human mind. We were told that this would lead to people becoming "clear" - a sort of superhumanity for the coming age.

But what in fact happened? Instead of a new generation of clear people, the snakes in the unconscious seemed to writhe into ever tighter knots. The techniques grew more complex and bizarre and the practitioners themselves grew paranoid. The movement became crazy.

Some people realised the essential value of the basic ideas and left before things got too bad. For example, a couple who founded The Process. They were very intelligent people out to avoid the same mistakes - and yet their own movement turned crazy, as did several other offshoots of Scientology.

It is as if the very desire to "clear" and control the wilderness of the unconscious jungle will lead to a furious reaction. This is so predictable that, whenever I hear of some new movement promising to unlock inner potential and bestow mastery, I am confident that the movement will eventually turn totalitarian or collapse into crazed civil war.

Isn't this supposed to be still the age of reason? even when we feel crazy we now know enough about human emotion, genetic factors, environmental conditioning and psychology to explain it all away. Yet rave parties, pop concerts and political demonstrations unleash as much if not more hysteria than the world has ever witnessed.

When I saw the film of the Doors, I recognised so much of the myth of Dionysus in the figure of Jim Morrison. Sure enough, one of the characters in it shook his hand and said "I have played music with Dionysus". I then read the Penguin Classics version of the play The Bacchae and was very struck by what was said in the introduction to that work.

Unlike Uranus, Dionysus was not an ancient god. In fact he seems to have arrived very late - at a time when Greece was becoming very civilised. The suggestion was made that Dionysus arose as a shadow to civilisation - his worship was an ecstatic rebellion against the growing bureaucratic control of the state and the arrogance of humanity's emerging consciousness.

That was what made the myth so relevant to today. Once again the principle of Control is making huge gains - we *know* so much - and at the same time as it turns us into a flock of passive, controlled machines it evokes a primal wildness that threatens to overturn the whole of civilisation. The greater the control and the further we are from Nature, the crazier the reaction becomes - as in our most sophisticated modern cities. The more conscious the control, the greater the disorder it seems to invoke.

The normal tendency seems to be to identify with control and to project the wildness - people in England will talk in awed tones about the latest madness sweeping America; people in the country tremble at the thought of inner city violence; townsfolk stay in their cars rather than walk in the country alone or at night. I suspect that even the football hooligan - the terror of suburban Britain - has a sense that they are only playing at violence and that there are others who...

In fact I have a fantasy about turning up looking frightfully prim and proper in a pub where football hooligans are tanking up for a battle. I know the temptation to play up to someone who looks game to be shocked - half the tabloid press' coverage of ultraviolence owes its existence to outrageous claims made by kids wanting to be quoted in the papers - so in my fantasy they would let rip with all the "yer we're gonna kill the wops" "can't wait ter smash a few faces" and all that. Whereupon I would turn to them with silky smoothness saying "perhaps I can help" and start handing out several tons of high velocity automatic rifles, bazookas, hand grenades, nerve gas rocket launchers and so on. At which point the kids go pale with shock and splutter "you can't do that!"

The pleasure in this fantasy is this: we were playing the game of control versus wildness, me being the gentleman and evoking their loutishness in response. I then crack the game by behaving so outrageously that they are now forced into shocked disapproval. They were hooligans on the outside, preparing to put the boot into my sensibilities, whereas I have turned out to be an inner hooligan who puts the boot into their expectations of a gentleman. Get it?

You see I believe that the hooligan actually needs an inner sense of decency and fair play in order to be so good at outwardly rebelling against it. The wildest yobs often grow into the strictest disciplinarians.

The object of the example is to show that taking sides in a cosmic battle is not such a simple business as it seems. If you take sides with law and order you may encourage the very opposite.

Avoid the simple idea that the State was a smoothly funtioning, civilised machine into which Dionysus burst like a wild raging animal. On the contrary, Dionysus took the form of a very gentle and effete young man - the hippy, not the beast or guerilla fighter. His religion took the women of the town out into the country where they forgot their duties and returned to blissful communion with nature. It was only when Pentheus sent out the soldiers to haul them back that the women turned nasty and feral, tearing up animals and men with their bare hands.

Dionysus Himself was a very still and quiet figure who seemed to invoke madness around Him. Pentheus himself goes crazy - the madness is latent in the government and Dionysus seems merely to release it.

Control justifies its dominion by positing insane wildness as its opposite. That is in itself mad, because the true opposite of control is acceptance.

We may no longer bow down before a notion of perfection in

this relativistic Aeon of Horus, however perfection has been with us for a long time and it is still rooted in our unconscious minds. No longer worshipped it turns into a monster - the perfect ideal of Uranus is the monster it creates - and we fear it. As children we imagined that grown ups were perfect, they never did anything naughty like having sex. That once inspiring ideal is now a tyrant as we become adolescent - we don't want to give up sex and be perfect, boring adults.

Society actually *fears* Utopia, because it is perfect. New York, for example, is such a civilised place that its citizens *need* all the violence and crime in order to prove to themselves that this isn't really heaven. Try telling New Yorkers that you feel safe walking their streets and they act quite hurt. Centuries of puritan tradition believing that life has to be a struggle is all you need to make sure people will continue to create hell around themselves rather than fall into perfection. Utopia, everyone insists, would be sterile - forgetting that if it was sterile it would not be Utopia.

The Aeon of Horus challenges us to become gods. That is scary because we have for centuries insisted that god is perfect. Our sense of perfection is the greatest monster of all, so we kill it whenever it is likely to be realised. Our revolutions are self-defeating because the game of balancing control and acceptance is still infected with the old difficulty of idealism versus reality. The game is once more a battle.

Conclusion

What the hell am I rattling on about? It's something to do with reasons why some of us are not frightfully good at making things happen - and perhaps we can blame it all on the gods...

Anyway, I got a bit carried away as I always do on my last chapter. This may not look like a last chapter, but something went wrong with the otherwise historical sequence and the 13th essay was missing so I decided to write this to fill the gap and give the book a nice title.

Whoopee! almost the end of this volume. I'm so grateful to Revelations 23 Press for playing Gaia to my Uranus - and I promise to try really hard not to kill the book by getting too cranky.

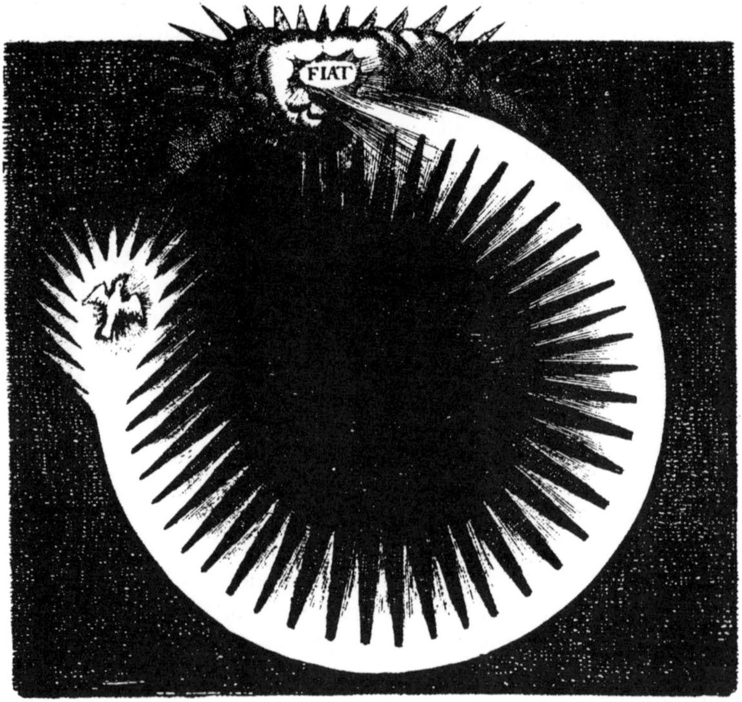

Let there be light by Robert Fludd

14 - THE MAGICIAN AND THE HIGH PRIEST

This is the other version of the Minister for Technology and the Pope story which I referred to in Words Made Flesh.

This version continues the story forward until our present day, concentrating on developments within the virtual reality of this universe rather than focussing on the metauniverse as the original story did. It is written in a much more obscure "sci-fi" style because I cut it very short for a short story competition. Perhaps the less said about that the better...

In the beginning the word was "RUN".

In the four dimensional continuum ten to the power of seventy eight randomly distributed hydrogen atoms were subject to the laws of particle physics, and began imperceptibly to drift together under mutual attraction. As they came closer the forces grew stronger and they fell ever faster towards a centre which was as yet nothing, but which would become all.

Thus was unity born from chaos.

That centre was the womb of chaos and it was, momentarily, all of chaos as the atoms collided, coalesced fused and gave forth blazing light. Now hydrogen was no longer alone; from it was created a heavier, more complex companion in helium.

Thus was duality born from chaos.

Yet duality was pre-existent in spirit, for all this was witnessed by two: the Knowing One who knew all secrets, and who revealed them to his lord the Holy One. Together they passed everywhere and saw all; the Knowing One was exultant, but the Holy One was aghast.

From the fire were born nebulae, from the nebulae were born suns, around the suns were formed planets; and the planets cooled.

Thus was the many born from primal chaos.

The Knowing One said to the Holy One "This universe is my gift to you", and the Holy One knew fear and doubt.

They were standing on one planet watching its sun sink crimson through a poison atmosphere beyond a leaden sea. "This is where it will happen", he said, "the conditions are perfect. Wait and see". The Holy One studied him and wondered what moved him. "I will leave you alone now, just to prove it."

Hearing those words, the Holy One sensed danger and decided to take pre-emptive action.

There is a tablet, it is square. A finger touches it - the finger of the Holy One. Where the finger touches, light blazes forth to reveal a word engraved upon the tablet: "HOLD".

The light reflects on the gleaming surface of a red sphere as hands grasp the sphere and lift it to uncover the silver hair on the head of the Holy One.

He goes to the door of the small chamber, locks it on the inside and stands a moment in silent prayer. Then he goes over to the body of the Knowing One, removes the similar red helmet and places it to one side, examines the face closely, returns to his couch, replaces his own helmet, lies back and touches another button. The word "RUN" now shines as the word "HOLD" vanishes.

Thus was the Knowing One cast out of heaven for his pride, and locked in the illusion of matter.

On discovering his fate, the Knowing One was furious and perplexed. The Holy One replied that one who knew so much could surely deduce the reason for his punishment, but perhaps lacked the courage to admit it? The Knowing One raged but, because only the Holy One had the power to return to heaven, he had to be subtle: he pleaded that this universe was the innocent gift of a loving servant. The Holy One replied that he now had an eternity to prove it; and he renamed him Lucifer, the Cunning One, because he had revealed much.

Together they watched life spontaneously evolve within that sea. Lucifer was exultant and the Holy One aghast. Millions of years rolled by and they witnessed a cruel planet growing green and fruitful. They saw slithery things emerge, evolve, grow legs, grow fur and grow beautiful. Out of beauty evolved humour, and Lucifer laughed at the antics of the apes. Alone or together, they passed freely among these creatures.

One day they stood on a grassy slope and watched a hairy hominid at play, endlessly banging stone upon stone, "like a soulless machine" in the bitter words of the Holy One. But the creature produced a spark and made fire; and Lucifer turned triumphantly to his master and added "a machine that knows what it is doing!"

The Holy One wept inwardly as they crouched to share the fire.

From that day Lucifer trod carefully and tried to please. As they came and went among the people of this world, he watched his master's reactions closely. There was much to delight them in this innocent world, but The Holy One seemed fretful, suspicious.

To the Holy One this seeming penance was more sinister than open opposition; he felt undercurrents of evil. Then it happened: as he appeared casually to some tribesmen, they fell back in fear, threw themselves at his feet, and named him "God". He vanished in a clap of thunder, and raged after Lucifer.

Lucifer too showed fear. It had seemed only fair to share the knowledge of their creation with the creatures; he had only told the truth. God spat out the word "fair" like viper's venom and held Lucifer by the throat till all was revealed.

By stepping to and fro in time it had been possible to speak to the fairest of the womenfolk in every tribe. No harm was done, for it was easy to turn back time to undo this innocent act... But he was suddenly speaking to emptiness.

The High Priest jabs the "HOLD" button and whips off his helmet. Stepping over to his Magician's comatose body he checks it cursorily, then paces up and down. He tries to pray, hopelessly. Then he returns to the console and hesitates before saying "I wish to create a program".

A soft voice replies "Then please answer the following questions. One, what is the name of the intended program?"

The High Priest scratches his head in confusion.

"If you are unaccustomed to programming, may I explain that this name is a simple reference for your own convenience: any word or phrase, not commencing with a numeral, and of not more than ten syllables."

"Er, Michael?" he shrugs, and "URMICHAEL?" appears on the screen.

"No, just 'Michael'".

"Now please give a brief functional description of the program."

The High Priest strokes his chin like one milking his memory, then begins. "A program to enforce 'read only' access to the low level software so as to inhibit reversals of experienced time...."

Lucifer hit a wall of fire, a flaming blade that hacked his consciousness into blazing shards. Tumbling backwards, he struggled to disentangle subjective effects from probable causes. He recognised to his horror a thoroughly amateurish piece of tampering with the software. It was his turn to rage after God. The people huddled together for shelter as the tempests shrieked around them.

Lucifer called God a clumsy, meddling imbecile. Did he realise what he had done? Every single action on this universe lead to an endless chain of consequences, now there was no hope of undoing any of them. Limitless suffering had been unleashed. Detailed knowledge of the most intricate workings of this program was needed before anyone should dare experiment on it!

God had done what had to be done. After all these aeons was Lucifer still insisting that knowledge was the only relevant factor?

Lucifer screamed that he was talking about RESPONSIBILITY, and God replied that it had been worth waiting eight billion years to hear that word in this context.

What did God want? Lucifer would do anything to be released from this prison of illusion. It was no good answering such questions directly, because the trickster who could feign a universe would be infinitely skillful at feigning correct responses. God wanted truth of a different order from sheer knowledge: "look into your heart!"

"All I see is anger!"

"That is better than nothing!"

Shaking his head and retiring meekly, for God still held the key, Lucifer swore to himself that God would pay for his folly.

Thus was mankind cast out of Paradise.

There was famine, plague, war, flood, pestilence and tyranny. God struggled to spread enlightenment and hope, but learned caution in the face of mounting complexity. There were signs of sabotage: signs of Lucifer most subtly foiling his efforts, as if to ensure that mankind would visibly suffer the full consequences of God's involvement.

Worse by far were the acts of contrition: when Lucifer tried to win favour by helping mankind. He had faith in education: sharing the secrets of magic with men of influence, and never comprehending why they chose to use this knowledge to gain dominion over illusion, rather than to relieve suffering.

At such times God too yearned to end it all and return to heaven. "Is this really the same mind?" he wondered, "or has the scanner helmet misread the Magician's brain structure and modelled a demon in his place?"

Together as students they had signed a petition condemning the use of brain surgery on violent criminals, and the use of drugs for political ends; yet this Lucifer had been tampering with the software of a whole world, as if it were a toy, in order to create a false paradise. What had happened to conscience? Who was it that had risked his neck to attack the priesthood's missionary proselytising as an act of cultural genocide? Was it the same mind who now tried to teach savages the secrets of the universe? Had he ever had a conscience or had he simply been playing politics back in heaven?

There was less time to ponder such problems, now that life circumscribed the globe, and evil never slept. If education was the answer, then it had to be a moral education. As it was impossible to fully predict the consequences, it was clearly safest to isolate those being educated; and the only justifiable solution was to find a tribe that had nothing to lose: a tribe in slavery and under the threat of genocide.

There was suddenly no alternative but to commit one of those acts of conscience that Lucifer would call "irresponsible meddling". Seeing the rich girl approaching, God remained invisible but threw a small pebble so that it landed among the rushes. There was a splash, the baby cried out, and Pharaoh's daughter looked to see what the noise was.

Thus did the children of Israel became the chosen race.

With the passing of time the system gained inertia.

As matter, then life, then intelligence, and now social structures evolved, the equations grew more complex and the computations longer, so that subjective time in the inner universe ran slower relative to time in heaven. As the second law of thermodynamics spread disorder there were ever-growing demands on memory, so objective time in the inner universe also ran slower. It became increasingly difficult to defy the 'laws of nature' and act directly as the universe of meaning became more tightly knit.

On the other hand there was greater feedback in the system. In early days a miraculous intervention would become a tribe's jealously guarded secret; now new empires were appearing whose structure allowed wider communication. Action in one area could now be transmitted across continents, and could even be amplified and exaggerated in the process.

A new approach was needed, and God discussed it with Lucifer.

Lucifer explained that it would be madness.

Apart from the sheer limitation of incarnating in this hellish world, there was the time factor. Because of the relationship with their bodies in what he chose to call "the real world", they had been able to endure many billions of years here, as in a dream. But to incarnate would be to subject oneself totally to this experience of time: each year of incarnate life would weigh like a full year, a year of hell.

Hearing this, God felt even more certain that he must do it, and still Lucifer failed to understand.

Thus was God made man.

Christ bit his tongue to stifle screams as the nails drove into the palms of his hands. Even now Lucifer was whispering to him, begging him to give up and get them both out of this world: "one little miracle, and we could both be back in the real world enjoying a nice cup of coffee."

Lucifer triumphed: he heard the words "my God, why hast thou forsaken me", and knew he'd won at last.

His campaign had been conceived twenty years ago in real time, when development began on a revolutionary computer of unprecedented power. He had realised that it offered the first ever chance to model the entire creation of a universe from randomised initial conditions, assuming only the known laws of physics. For the first time the court magicians could prove something long argued with the priests: namely that such a universe would develop life, intelligence, humanity, and would therefore prove God and spirit to be totally redundant concepts.

A stunning triumph, and one that would mark the end of the priests' political dominance.

This triumph left Lucifer in despair, and he could not understand why. There was a sense only of anticlimax.

His victory had been a forgone conclusion even as they first entered this universe. He had wanted to leave the Priest to it, and get straight back to the real world to seek some other novelty to distract a bored mind - for winning the battle of a lifetime would leave a big hole in one's sense of purpose.

Instead he'd been trapped in his own game, and spent millions of years toying with an illusion created for someone else's edification. Observing the increasingly humanistic colouring of the Priest's ideas as time passed, merely spelled out the inevitability of his defeat.

So dejected was Lucifer, that he fell on his knees at the feet of Christ Deceased, confessed everything and begged for a return to heaven. He even promised to erase the program and tell no-one what he had done.

To his amazement, Christ laughed as he had not laughed for aeons.

You don't forget the death of God that easily. But anyway, Christ had found God reborn: in Lucifer's mind! Or, more strictly, in the unconscious mind of the Magician.

The Magician had intended to convince the High Priest that there could be no qualitative distinction between this godless, mechanistic world and the real world they lived in. Aeons of living with this model, and one short lifetime actually incarnate within it, had convinced the High Priest that there was indeed no distinction. Therefore God was dead, a fallacy to be outgrown by intellectual advancement. But although he himself had felt that distinction between 'real' and 'artificial' worlds being eroded, Lucifer had not...

Lucifer consistently made an unconscious distinction between this world, which he was perfectly prepared to destroy once it had served his purpose, and the 'real' world, in which he behaved as a man of feeling and conscience. Lucifer, as programmer, knew too much about this world to give it any validity. His very knowledge had formed a barrier to feeling.

Trapped within Lucifer's unconscious mind, their God had declared this world a godless abomination. Lucifer's very knowledge had made him a devil to this world.

Christ realised that this was the lesson that had to be understood before the helmet was replaced to update the Magician's neural network, and so release Lucifer from what he had himself prejudged to be an illusion.

Christ laughed once more and said that, now God had risen again for him, so would God rise again for this world.

Thus God, as Christ, did.

It was a turning point although, after eight billion years, one could not expect the turn to be fast or dramatic.

Lucifer made some progress towards understanding; Christ assured him he would finally get the point if he would only incarnate as the Antichrist; but Lucifer shuddered at the thought of incarnating, and put off the dreaded day.

And Christ had another worry: he recalled the Magician once claiming that programming was still an art: however clear the mathematical structure, one could still recognise the hand of its creator in a program.

Had the Magician programmed rather more of his unconscious into this world than he'd intended?

The High Priest keys "HOLD", removes his helmet and goes over to the Magician's body. He searches around the couch, finds the briefcase, takes the Magician's keys, and opens it. He is searching for something he noticed this morning in real time. It is gone.

He frowns, then runs his hands over the Magician's clothing. He has found it: an automatic pistol. It is loaded.

The High Priest takes the cartridges one by one, puts them to his mouth, bites each bullet and tugs it free. He pockets the bullets, replaces the blank cartridges in the magazine, replaces the pistol, returns to his couch, replaces his helmet, lies back, and keys "RUN".

Christ has an appointment with Lucifer.

"What are they doing in that bunker?"

"Wait and see."

The desert sun blazed down as they waited among the cacti that fringed the compound. This universe had grown very complex, Christ realised. He who had once raised mountains and parted the Red Sea would now find it hard even to create a rainstorm. But if he did, it would be instantly recorded worldwide. Lucifer was speaking again.

"But the real understanding came when I realised WHY I wanted to commit suicide. The victory was hollow because all along I hadn't been fighting the priesthood, but the warlords! They're the real enemy. Do you know what this computer is officially for? It's been developed for the army! The greatest achievement of all time being handed over as a plaything for dumb soldiers and stupid politicians! Rather than face that directly, I must've decided that a world without religion would be a world without a devil, and therefore a world without war. Look! there it goes..."

Christ turned and witnessed the first atom bomb being exploded. He sighed "So, if these people destroy themselves, you get your cup of coffee early. Otherwise we stay till they create their own universes and learn for themselves what we now know. By that time this world will be running so slowly that we'll be due to leave anyway. Either way, you and I go back to heaven united in the name of peace and hope - ok?"

The digitised simulacra of a High Priest and a Court Magician shook hands and embraced in the desert as the mushroom cloud obscured the sun.

MORE FROM R23 THE MOUSEHOLE...

*... **Revelations 23 Press & The Mouse That Spins** presents two more spiritually uplifting reasons why you should murder a rich uncle or rob a bank to raise some ready cash this year.*

*Thanks to a long-needed injection of publishing competence from the **Revelations 23 Press**, there will be more books limping off the press shortly*

NEWS! NEWS!

TMTS DISREPUTABLE - AN IMPORTANT NEW IMPRINT FROM THE MOUSE THAT SPINS!

The Mouse That Spins.

... a name that marks a new dawning in man's relentless quest for mastery of the written word.

... a name synonymous with the finest in key leading-edge concepts packaged in the latest state-of-the-art Bound Off-line Optical-input Knowledge Systems (BOOKS).

... a name that transformed one corner of a bedroom in a fourth floor flat in the ancient capital of England into an International Centre of Publishing Excellence.

... a name that has senior players in the world's major financial markets appearing at work dressed as mice and speaking with squeaky voices in a desire to acquire honour by association.

In short - just a name.

The Mouse That Spins' dedicated team of publishing professionals - boasting no less than ten man-years of occasional publishing experience between him - is proud to announce the creation of an important new imprint to head its thrust into seminal occult niche markets of the 21st century... *TMTS DISREPUTABLE.*

"In presenting *TMTS DISREPUTABLE* to our public" explains Ramsey Dukes, Managing Editor in the European Division of the Magickal Subsection of the Contemporary Topics Department, "we aim to deploy the full weight of The Mouse's considerable financial, technical and creative resources in our determination to bring to the world a product just that little bit worse than anyone else's

WHAT I DID IN MY HOLIDAYS - essays on black magic, satanism, devil worship and other niceties. By Ramsey Dukes.

If you liked Blast Your Way, you will be ready to kill for a copy of What I Did - Volume 3 of Ramsey Dukes' collected essays now being prepared for publication. This volume brings the corpus right up to date.

Volume 1 (Uncle Ramsey's Bumper Book of Magick Spells and other essays on science and magic) will follow later because it contains earlier stuff that was never put onto computer disk and so needs to be keyed in.

Forthcoming from R23 & *TMTS DISREPUTABLE:*

THE NAKED, SHOCKING TRUTH BEHIND THE INTERNATIONAL SATANIC CONSPIRACY

No question was more hotly debated by the International Satanic Executive in the mid 70s than this: should they come out into the open, or should they continue to corrupt civilisation from behind the scenes?

No voice will be better remembered than that of the Honourable Hugo C StJ l'Estrange, Minister for Moral Decline and grand old man of British Satanism, arguing that the election of Margaret Thatcher was a clear signal that his country was weary of 60s idealism and was crying out for True Evil to lead the way.

Because of this stirring appeal, Satanism went public - with Hugo l'Estrange's "Satanists Diary" appearing as a regular column in Aquarian Arrow. No-one would be so rash as to deny the worldwide moral and spiritual decline that has resulted.

In this volume we will be presenting the entire unexpurgated Satanist's Diary in all its evil glory. Here you can meet such vile personages as: Dr Sigismund Galganspiel, Minister for Absolute Evil; Miss Florence Dashwood, of the Cheltenham Ladies' Lilith Association; the Very Irreverend Dr Eival B Myeghud DSat, DipDiab, MDem Bishop of the Church of Eternal Damnation; Ernest Synner, Student Representative... and other entities too revolting for words.

THE HELLGATE CHRONICLES - by Hugo l'Estrange - a DISREPUTABLE book from Revelations 23 Press and The Mouse That Spins

REVELATIONS 23 PRESS

Revelations 23 Press is an autonomous manifestation ov thee T.O.P.Y. philosophy in ACTION. Making Data Flesh for those with thee desire to touch themselves. Thee first three Volumes ov Five in our Occultural series are now available. The Book of Results, Magical Incenses and Blast Your Way (this volume), thee first three volumes in the series deal with very different principles ov Magickal theory and practice but they are all unique Individual volumes in thee series, all cut away thee dead flesh ov thee old grimoires with vigour and wisdom allowing thee lifeforce (Magick) to return to the source, thee Individual. Revelations 23 Press is pleased to announce thee release ov thee titles, which are produced to the highest standard. Details are also given on forthcouming editions to thee series, thee release dates will be transmitted through Thee T.O.P.Y. World Nett-Work.

MAGICAL INCENSES
by Dave Lee.

This book is the most informative and practical volume on the subject that you're likely to come across, it provides the necessary know-how to start making Magical Incense for ritual, celebration and meditation. All the ingredients are fully explained, over 100 of them, and over 70 recipes are given. For those who wish to formulate their own recipes - comprehensive tables of correspondences are included. Magical Incenses is a ground breaking book, suitable for both the complete beginner as well as the advanced ritualist, every aspect of the subject is discussed and explained in full, giving for the first time all the information needed to approach and study the art of making and using Magical Incenses. While it may be easier to burn a joss stick from a corner shop for a ritual, this is just a case of cutting corners and doing without, with the wealth of information provided in this book you need never do without again.

A5-Perfectbound
ISBN 1 874171 01 7
£5.50 - UK
£5.75 - Europe
£6.00 - Rest of World

THE BOOK OF RESULTS by Ray Sherwin.

The Book of Results is an Ingeious contribution to the Pratice and Theory of Sigils, explaining and expanding the practices and principles developed by the great English Mage Austin Osman Spare. The Book of Results explains, in plain English, the sleight of mind techniques of Sigilisation, as well as full rituals, banishing techniques, mantras and dervish whirling, all of which create the most powerful rites. This book is a landmark in the history of Magickal thought. Ray Sherwin's 15 years of experience and experiments are clearly reflected, and will be of great interest to those new to the subject-as well as those familiar with the Magickal Process of Sigilisation. A Book for RESULTS.

" Buy it. Study it and Use it. The ratio of practising magickians to collectors of magickal books is probably 1:1000, hopefully this book will rectify the situation" - **Peter J. Carroll**

This edition of The Book of Results has been specially revised and expanded for Revelations 23 Press.

A5-Perfectbound
ISBN 1 874171 00 9
£5.00 - UK
£5.50 - Europe
£6.00 - Rest of World.

Make all cheques\I.M.O\Postal Orders

REVELATIONS 23 PRESS
c/o T.O.P.Y. STATION 23
P.O.BOX 687
HALFWAY
SHEFFIELD
S19 5UX
UK